The Crime Analysis
Laboratory Manual for
Applied Learning in

CRIME MAPPING &
DATA-DRIVEN EXERCISES

Dr. Brian Kelly

Kendall Hunt
publishing company

Kendall Hunt
publishing company

www.kendallhunt.com
Send all inquiries to:
4050 Westmark Drive
Dubuque, IA 52004-1840

Contents

Section 1 Applied Learning for Crime Mapping

LAB EXERCISES

Section 2 Applied Learning Framework for 'Rate' Typology—Crime Rate

LAB EXERCISES

Introduction

The Crime Analysis Laboratory Manual for Applied Learning in Crime Mapping and Data-driven Exercises is designed to accompany a one-semester, college course encompassed within the concept of Geographic Information Systems (GIS), in particular, the aspects of Crime Mapping, as observed in many academic programs whose framework focuses on crime justice, police administration, and crime analysis. The impetus utilized incorporates higher education thru applied learning, whereas basic competencies acquired through lecture, and most importantly, hands-on practice, may be attributed to real scenarios within professional industries.

This manual presents detailed functional information for lab-based exercises pertaining to the multiple forms of crime analysis, via the utilization of mapping software, often recreating scenarios through an interface, based on tabular (in this case crime data), and geographic data, respectively. Students in these courses are pursuing careers in a law enforcement profession, or professions engulfed within data-driven or predictive components, including where vitality is observed through usage of GIS operations.

The analysis of qualitative and quantitative data is also a primary element, as seen throughout each lab exercise. While the manual is not technologically oriented aside from the software used to complete the labs, it provides a solid foundation for any student interested in learning more about the crime mapping, and data-driven policing, coupled with the overarching categories of Crime Analysis.

Background

First let's acknowledge that Crime Analysis is multidimensional. Whenever anything is multidimensional, by in large, it can allow for some positive attributes and uses within our society. Hence, Crime Analysis includes its own set of factors, whereas: (1) Crime Analysis is a Concept. Concepts are specific areas of subject matter, often embedded in blocks of instruction, or carefully designed curriculum possessing modules containing assessments, which allow a learner to acquire this knowledge to be applied in real-life scenarios; (2) Crime Analysis is a process. Any process allows for research-oriented techniques to be used to examine and interpret data which may be vital to police agencies and their communities.

© majson/Shutterstock.com

These processes include the analysis of crime and criminals, crime victims, crime disorder, community concerns to be presented by agencies through interpreted data, traffic issues, and internal police operations. The results of these processes allow the data to support criminal investigation and prosecution, patrol activities, crime prevention and reduction, problem solving, and the evaluation of police efforts.

Impetus and Rationale

As a university professor who consistently instructs curriculum attributable to the hands-on aspect of this manual (Crime Mapping, alongside the overarching parameters of Crime Analysis) I chose to create this laboratory manual because I perceived that a gap existed within the hands-on practice of crime mapping and GIS-oriented curriculum, as observed within many undergraduate college programs who offer this specialized material in their course catalogs. Furthermore, I felt that the current state of custom-create content required to assess students when instructing these courses, especially when a laboratory requirement is established for mapping aptitude, is not readily available for engaging instruction, from an applied learning standpoint. This of course excludes the many tutorials and samples offered in governmental and private sector guides.

The primary resource for this course's applied learning components, as correlated with the laboratory exercises, is the software manufactured by ESRI, titled ArcGIS, specifically ArcGIS Online.

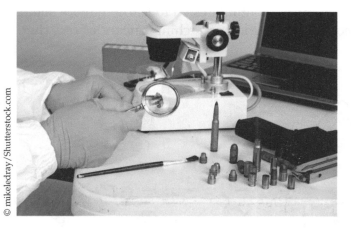
© mikeledray/Shutterstock.com

ESRI does not create content or subscribe to one specific industry. This is primarily due to the fact that many industries are essentially data driven, not just Law Enforcement. Furthermore, dozens of industries do use GIS mapping software to manage projects, establish necessary countermeasures, as well as to create tools to allow for presentation, and the delivery of data, for a more visual format. However, for a more robust examination and hands-on learning process, I feel ArcGIS Online is imperative for crime mapping within the college classroom at the undergraduate level, in particular.

Applied Learning for Crime Mapping

The lab exercises within this section are designed to increase competency with GIS mapping software, while simultaneously allowing for the interpretations of data through analysis, without performing statistical calculations. I have designed each lab for Crime Mapping using qualitative themes, yet incorporating a multitude of data categories, in particular, as applied to GIS systems for map formulation. These themes are crime categories or geographic data concepts.

Many of the crimes observed throughout this manual include a multijurisdictional approach encompassed around the recognition of a simple fact: Any type of crime may occur anywhere throughout the world. These include: Drug Crimes and Narcotics Trafficking, Missing Persons, Terrorism, Violent Crimes, and other crimes categorized by the Federal Bureau of Investigation's Uniformed Crime Reports. This content allows for the examination of Tabular Data (Crime Data) reported and generated by agencies and third parties.

Other mapping exercises do not always include crime data, yet adhere to law enforcement agencies, and other aspects police work, or scenarios that impact society. Nonetheless, I am referring to geographic data such as schools, places of worship, commercial and residential properties, and other environments which are not required to be formulated and categorized using statistics, in and of themselves. I encourage instructors and students to take advantage of the opportunity to learn by practice, sparked by the capabilities of the software interface and components when making a map, using ArcGIS Online. ArcGIS Online allows for an explanation of data, through the utilization of Layers. The exercises endorse the upload of data, the opportunity to manipulate the data in a positive way to complete each task, and conclude with an overall analysis when responding to the questions in each lab exercise. An understanding and recognition of what in fact is being observed through relevant data will force a time-effective set of actions to be performed. Each exercise may enhance ones'aptitude pertaining to the software usage, and understanding the themes of the data sets used within each layer.

Quick Procedural Practice

Once logged in to the ArcGIS Online platform, the operator will choose to "Make a Map." Upon clicking and selecting this section the operator is directed to a Map interface. Important tools are:

A) The right-side toolbar which allows entry area to select a jurisdiction or geographic area;
B) The left-side integration which allow a user to "Add" and "Search for 'Layers";
C) The Content Area, which exhibits the Layer(s) the user uploaded to the interface, while also verifying the data through using symbols on the map being created;
D) The components observed within each Layer title, such as "Show Table" and "Change Style." By in large, these items encompass data which contribute to an imperative concept known as Temporal Analysis, as observed in many incidents of crime;
E) The user can create a map and recognize data represented by also using the traditional "Legend" to make some determinations, in conjunction with the data from the "Show Table" icon.
F) When using the Legend, click the first icon in the layer to view the legend, next to "Show Table." I am referring to the icon positioned all the way to the right of the left-hand column. It is represented by the three (3) consecutive dots, and will display the words, "More Options."
G) Once this is selected, a pop-up window will appear, and the user may scroll down, and observe "Show Item Details." This area will allow the user to further understand the data scenario currently in progress.

Lastly, to support the concepts of a map relevant to gauging proximity and recognizing Spatial Analysis, a measuring tool is recommended to be used, as seen in the primary toolbar above each map.

SECTION 1

Applied Learning for Crime Mapping

© Sudowoodo/Shutterstock.com

Synopsis of Lab-Theme

Lab Exercise 1 utilizes the state of Florida, and the city of Miami, as the primary jurisdiction. This map contains layers which include data representing Sexual Predators in the city of Miami, as well as Sexual Predators who also reside in areas that are within 2,500 ft of public schools. Lab Exercise 1 aims to also focus on an approach using Strategic Crime Analysis, due to the nature of the type of criminal offender exhibited in the layers, and on the map.

© Couperfield/Shutterstock.com

Table 1

Layer #	Layer Name	Data Type
One	Sexual Predator	Crime and Geographic
Two	Sexual predator within 2,500 ft of Public Schools	Crime and Geographic

Operational Lab-Tasks

This map will include geographic and criminal-oriented data, within the state of Florida, in particular the city of Miami, and its subsections. Sexual Predators within this jurisdiction are the primary data feature. Also, Sexual Predators within a specific distance from schools are utilized. Sexual Predators within certain proximity of learning institutions where minor children are located are used to build sex offender residency restriction zones in most states within our nation under state and federal laws.

Next, the following operational tasks using the capability features of ArcGIS Online will need to be completed, as seen below:

1. Enter Miami, Florida in the right toolbar
2. Left Column Toolbar: Click "Add"

3. See Dropdown Menu: Click "Search for Layers"
4. Type: Sexual Predator
    a. Scroll down, then add the following "Layers":
        1. Sex Predator
        2. Sexual Predator within 2,500 ft of public schools
5. If necessary, alter the symbol shape and color for any Layer using "Change Style"
6. Review all relevant data for each layer by clicking "Show Table," prior to formulating and submitting your responses

Once all Layers are added, your map should appear as seen below:

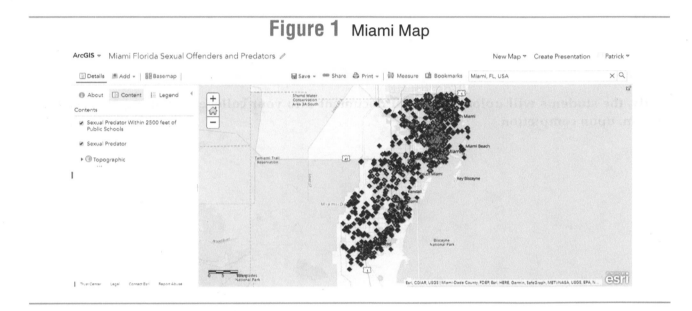

Figure 1   Miami Map

Part A

Students will respond accordingly to the following questions on this document, using the data provided.

1. What color eyes does Felipe Gonzalez possess?
2. How many offenders are there?
3. How many predators are there?
4. Name all of the possible "Status" these individuals can possess?
5. Who is the shortest Predator in height?
6. Who is the heaviest offender?
7. How many offenders live in Miami Gardens?
8. Is this entire data set "Registered" as a Sex Offender? Yes or no and why?
9. How far is offender 5773 from 5174?
10. Do 5773 and 5174 possess any commonalities? If yes, what are they?

Part B

Students will now perform an in-depth analysis with the current data in the layers uploaded to create a minimum of ten (10) questions on their own. Responses are only required if the instructor deems necessary:

1. Q1
2. Q2
3. Q3
4. Q4
5. Q5
6. Q6
7. Q7
8. Q8
9. Q9
10. Q10

Lastly, the students will upload this final document into your college's Learning Management System, upon completion.

ArcGIS Online

Synopsis of Lab-Theme

Lab Exercise 2 utilizes the state of Pennsylvania, as the primary jurisdiction. This map contains layers which include data representing Sex Offenders, Schools, Buffer of Schools, and Find Locations in Sex Offenders. Lab Exercise 2 aims to also focus on an approach using Strategic Crime Analysis, due to the nature of the type of criminal offender exhibited in the layers, as well as key geographic data, on the map.

Table 2

Layer #	Layer Name	Data Type
One	Sex Offenders	Crime and Geographic
Two	Schools	Geographic
Three	Buffer of Schools	Geographic
Four	Find Locations in Sex Offenders	Geographic

Operational Lab-Tasks

This map will include geographic and criminal-oriented data, within the state of Pennsylvania. Sexual offenders within this jurisdiction are the primary data feature. Also, Sexual Offenders within a specific distance from schools are utilized. Sexual Offenders within certain proximity of learning institutions where minor children are located are used to build sex offender residency restriction zones in most states within our nation under state and federal laws.

Next, the following operational tasks using the capability features of ArcGIS Online will need to be completed, as seen below:

1. Enter Pennsylvania in the right toolbar
2. Left Column Toolbar: Click "Add"
3. See Dropdown Menu: Click "Search for Layers"
4. Type: Sexual Offenders
   a. Scroll down, then add the following "Layers":
      1. Sex Offenders
      2. Buffer of Schools
      3. Schools
      4. Find Locations in Sex Offenders
5. If necessary, alter the symbol shape and color for any layer, using "Change Style"
6. Review all relevant data for each layer by clicking "Show Table," prior to formulating and submitting your responses

Once all Layers are added, your map should appear as seen below:

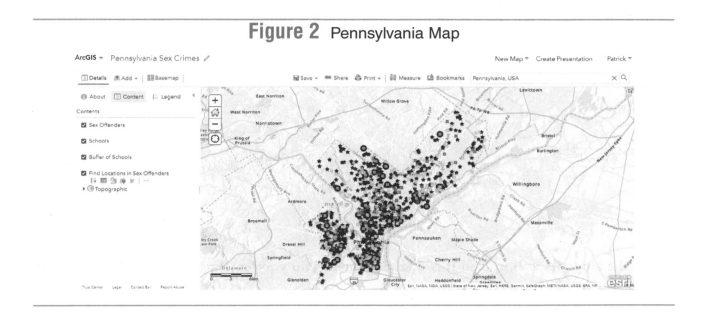

Figure 2 Pennsylvania Map

Part A

Students will respond accordingly to the following questions on this document, using the data provided.

1. How many sex offenders are within this data set?
2. How many sexually violent predators are there?
3. How many females are registered sex offenders in this data set?
4. How many offenders are Tier One?
5. How many offenders live on North Dover St?
6. Red symbols represent what?
7. How far is Ernest West from Dionte Grant?
8. How many sex offenders are female?
9. Which tier is Vladimir Lobo classified within?
10. How many cities are represented within this data set?

Part B

Students will now perform an in-depth analysis with the current data in the layers uploaded to create a minimum of ten (10) questions on their own. Responses are only required if the instructor deems necessary:

1. Q1
2. Q2
3. Q3
4. Q4
5. Q5
6. Q6
7. Q7
8. Q8
9. Q9
10. Q10

Lastly, the students will upload this final document into your college's Learning Management System, upon completion.

ArcGIS Online

© Sky and glass/Shutterstock.com

Synopsis of Lab-Theme

Lab Exercise 3 utilizes the state of Michigan, and the city of Detroit, as the primary jurisdiction. This map contains layers which include data representing Crime in the city of Detroit, as well as Fires which also require first response. Lab Exercise 3 aims to also focus on an approach using Tactical Crime Analysis, due to the nature of the type of incidents exhibited in the layers, and on the map.

© Jay Fog/Shutterstock.com

© Jeremiah Miller/Shutterstock.com

Table 3

Layer #	Layer Name	Data-Type
One	Fires Detroit 2015	Geographic
Two	Minn 2017 Crime Detroit	Crime

Operational Lab-Tasks

This map will include geographic and criminal-oriented data, within the state of Michigan, in particular the city of Detroit. Crimes and fires within this jurisdiction are the primary data feature, which allow for a closer examination of spatial and temporal analysis.

Next, the following operational tasks using the capability features of ArcGIS Online will need to be completed, as seen below:

1. Enter Detroit in the right toolbar
2. Left Column Toolbar: Click "Add"
3. See Dropdown Menu: Click "Search for Layers"
4. Type: Detroit crime
   a. Scroll down, then add the following "Layers":
      1. Fires Detroit 2015
      2. Minn 2017 Crime Detroit
5. If necessary, alter the symbol shape and color for any layer, using "Change Style"
6. Review all relevant data for each layer by clicking "Show Table," prior to formulating and submitting your responses

Once all Layers are added, your map should appear as seen below:

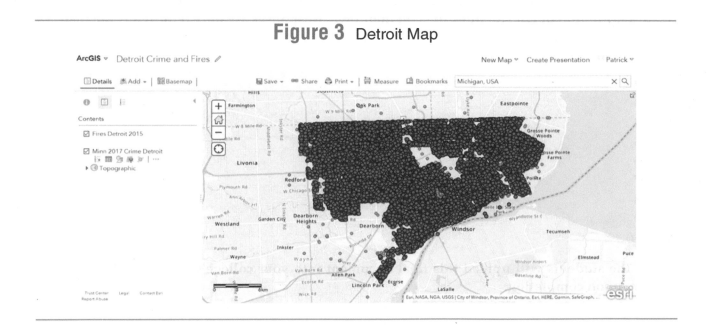

Figure 3 Detroit Map

Part A

Students will respond accordingly to the following questions on this document, using the data provided.

1. In 2015, how many fires occurred within Detroit?
2. In 2015, how many fires were documented as false alarms?
3. In 2015, how many incidents involved locations which were one or two family dwellings?
4. In 2014 how many calls were actually dispatched?
5. How many fires included civilian injuries?
6. How many crimes occurred in 2017?
7. How many stolen vehicle incidents occurred in 2017?
8. How many times was someone assaulted in 2017?
9. How many times was someone involved in a hit and run?
10. How many times was there a victim of larceny?

Part B

Students will now perform an in-depth analysis with the current data in the layers uploaded to create a minimum of ten (10) questions on their own. Responses are only required if the instructor deems necessary:

1. Q1
2. Q2
3. Q3
4. Q4
5. Q5
6. Q6
7. Q7
8. Q8
9. Q9
10. Q10

Lastly, the students will upload this final document into your college's Learning Management System, upon completion.

ArcGIS Online

4

SEATTLE

© Ray_of_Light/Shutterstock.com

Synopsis of Lab-Theme

Lab Exercise 4 utilizes the city of Seattle, Washington, as the primary jurisdiction. This map contains layers which include data representing a multitude of crime which occurred in this jurisdiction. This is reported crime, I will note. Lab Exercise 4 aims to also focus on an approach using Intelligence Crime Analysis, due to the nature of the type of criminal activity on the map.

© CineCam/Shutterstock.com

Table 4

Layer #	Layer Name	Data Type
One	Crime Seattle	Crime

Operational Lab-Tasks

This map will include criminal-oriented data, in particular, within the city of Seattle. Various crimes are featured throughout this data set highlighting temporal analysis.

Next, the following operational tasks using the capability features of ArcGIS Online will need to be completed, as seen below:

1. Enter Seattle, Washington, in the right toolbar
2. Left Column Toolbar: Click "Add"
3. See Dropdown Menu: Click "Search for Layers"
4. Type: Seattle Crime
    a. Scroll down, then add the following "Layers":
        1. Crime Seattle;
5. If necessary, alter the symbol shape and color for any layer, using "Change Style"
6. Review all relevant data for each layer by clicking "Show Table," prior to formulating and submitting your responses

Once all Layers are added, your map should appear as seen below:

Figure 4 ArcGIS Seattle Map

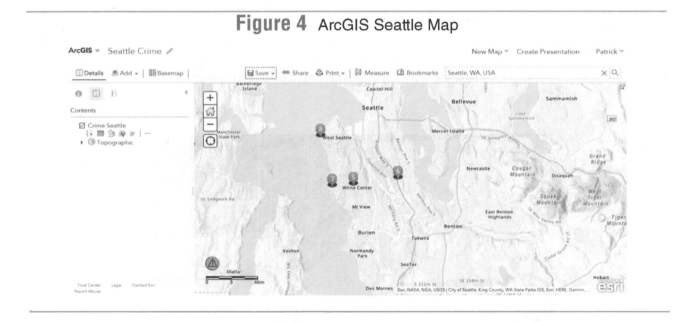

Part A

Students will respond accordingly to the following questions on this document, using the data provided.

1. What is the total time period for this data set in Seattle, Washington?
2. How many crime incidents occurred within this data set?
3. How many people trespassed in Seattle, per this data?
4. Which precinct was the busiest with calls, during this time?
5. Which Seattle neighborhood was the most active with crime?
6. Which month possessed the most crime within this data set?
7. How many motor vehicles were stolen within this data set?
8. Which precinct possessed the least amount of crime in this data set?
9. Which sector was the busiest within this data set?
10. Which police beat possesses the most documented incidents within this data set?

Part B

Students will now perform an in-depth analysis with the current data in the layers uploaded to create a minimum of ten (10) questions on their own. Responses are only required if the instructor deems necessary:

1. Q1
2. Q2
3. Q3
4. Q4
5. Q5
6. Q6
7. Q7
8. Q8
9. Q9
10. Q10

Lastly, the students will upload this final document into your college's Learning Management System, upon completion.

© Kursat Unsal/Shutterstock.com

Synopsis of Lab-Theme

Lab Exercise 5 utilizes the city of Denver, Colorado, as the primary jurisdiction. This map contains layers which include data representing various crimes over time, and each are recognized by the titles WinterAutoCrime, WinterViolentCrime, and Denvercrime. Tactical crime analysis is the focus.

© Daniel Jedzura/Shutterstock.com

Table 5

Layer #	Layer Name	Data Type
One	WinterAutoCrime	Crime
Two	WinterViolentCrime	Crime
Three	Denvercrime	Crime

Operational Lab-Tasks

This map will include crime within the city of Denver, as stated. Temporal aspects within this jurisdiction are the primary data feature for overall crime, amongst two other major categories of crime.

Next, the following operational tasks using the capability features of ArcGIS Online will need to be completed, as seen below:

1. Enter Denver, CO in the right toolbar
2. Left Column Toolbar: Click "Add"
3. See Dropdown Menu: Click "Search for Layers"
4. Type: Denver crime
   a. Scroll down, then add the following "Layers":
      1. WinterAutoCrime
      2. WinterViolentCrime
      3. Denvercrime
5. If necessary, alter the symbol shape and color for any layer, using "Change Style"
6. Review all relevant data for each layer by clicking "Show Table," prior to formulating and submitting your responses

Once all Layers are added, your map should appear as seen below:

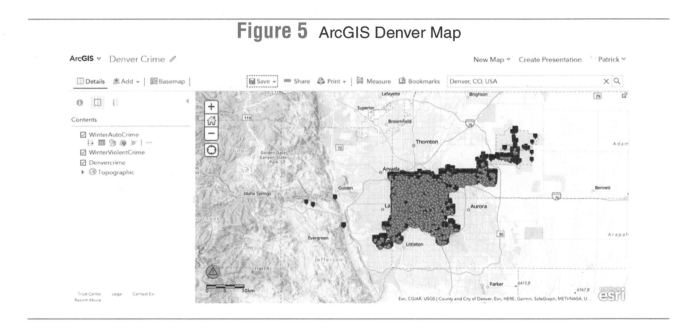

Figure 5 ArcGIS Denver Map

Part A

Students will respond accordingly to the following questions on this document, using the data provided.

1. How many times did someone criminally trespass in Denver?
2. How many times did a thief snatch a purse in Denver?
3. How many offenses occurred in 2017?
4. How many times did a perpetrator commit robbery on a street?
5. How many people fired a weapon into an occupied building?
6. How many traffic accidents occurred within this data set?
7. How many incidents of shoplifting occurred within this data set?
8. How many arrests were made for people fighting in public?
9. How many larcenies occurred within this data set?
10. Which month of the year possesses the most crime activity within this data set?

Part B

Students will now perform an in-depth analysis with the current data in the layers uploaded to create a minimum of ten (10) questions on their own. Responses are only required if the instructor deems necessary:

1. Q1
2. Q2
3. Q3
4. Q4
5. Q5
6. Q6
7. Q7
8. Q8
9. Q9
10. Q10

Lastly, the students will upload this final document into your college's Learning Management System, upon completion.

© krkt/Shutterstock.com

Synopsis of Lab-Theme

Lab Exercise 6 utilizes the city of Atlanta, as the primary jurisdiction. This map contains layers which include data representing an abundance of crime which was reported within a specific window of time. Lab Exercise 6 aims to also focus on an approach using Strategic Crime Analysis, due to the nature of the type of crimes exhibited in the layer, and on the map.

© TuckerBlade/Shutterstock.com

Table 6

Layer #	Layer Name	Data Type
One	Atlanta Crimes	Crime

Operational Lab-Tasks

This map will include criminal-oriented data, within the city of Atlanta, as discussed. A multitude of crime is to be examined, including violent crime, highlighting temporal and spatial factors.

Next, the following operational tasks using the capability features of ArcGIS Online will need to be completed, as seen below:

1. Enter Atlanta in the right toolbar
2. Left Column Toolbar: Click "Add"
3. See Dropdown Menu: Click "Search for Layers"
4. Type: Atlanta Crime
   a. Scroll down, then add the following "Layers":
      1. Atlanta Crimes
5. If necessary, alter the symbol shape and color for this layer, using "Change Style"
6. Review all relevant data for each layer by clicking "Show Table," prior to formulating and submitting your responses

Once all Layers are added, your map should appear as seen below:

Figure 6 ArcGIS Atlanta Map

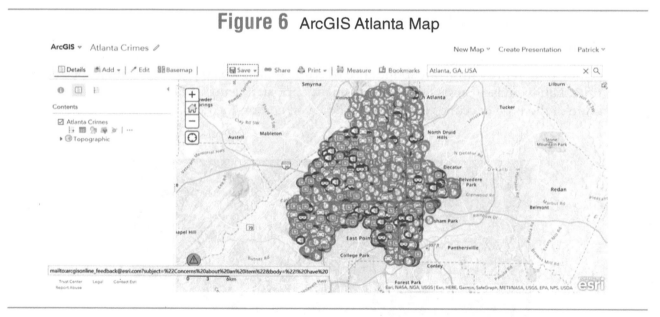

Part A

Students will respond accordingly to the following questions on this document, using the data provided.

1. How many crimes were committed in Atlanta, per this data?
2. What is the total window of time which this data set covers?
3. How many homicides were committed in Atlanta in 2012?
4. How many aggravated assaults were committed in Atlanta in 2016?
5. How many robberies were committed in Atlanta in 2013?
6. How many auto thefts were committed in Atlanta in 2012?
7. How many homicides were committed in Atlanta in 2015?
8. How many homicides were committed in Atlanta in 2014?
9. How many larcenies were committed in Atlanta in 2015?
10. How many homicides were committed in Atlanta in 2019?
11. How many vehicle thefts were committed in Atlanta in 2018?
12. How many robberies were committed in Atlanta in 2017?
13. How many aggravated assaults were committed in Atlanta in 2009?
14. How many homicides were committed in Atlanta in 2011?
15. How many vehicle thefts were committed in Atlanta in 2012?
16. How many homicides were committed in Atlanta in 2009?
17. How many robberies were committed in Atlanta in 2010?
18. How many aggravated assaults were committed in Atlanta in 2011?
19. How many times did a crime occur in Candler Park in 2012?
20. How many homicides were committed in Lenox in 2010?
21. How many crimes were committed Downtown in 2011?
22. How many crimes were committed in Wyngate in 2009?
23. How many crimes were committed in Virginia-Highland in 2019?
24. How many crimes were committed in Perkerson in 2012?
25. How many crimes were committed in Midtown in 2014?

Part B

Students will now perform an in-depth analysis with the current data in the layers uploaded to create a minimum of ten (10) questions on their own. Responses are only required if the instructor deems necessary:

1. Q1
2. Q2
3. Q3
4. Q4
5. Q5
6. Q6
7. Q7
8. Q8
9. Q9
10. Q10

Lastly, the students will upload this final document into your college's Learning Management System, upon completion.

ArcGIS Online

© Sky and glass/Shutterstock.com

Synopsis of Lab-Theme

Lab Exercise 7 utilizes the province of Quebec, Canada, specifically the city of Montreal, as the primary jurisdiction. This map contains layers which include data representing hot spots, essentially clusters of crime which signify possible patterns, and also intensity among that proximity. Montreal PDQ Boundaries Merged with SPVM 2017 Crime Stats, HOT SPOTS Montreal Crime Statistics 2015 to 2018, and Montreal Crime Statistics 2015 to 2018 will be utilized.

© meunierd/Shutterstock.com

Table 7

Layer #	Layer Name	Data Type
One	Montreal PDQ Boundaries Merged with SPVM 2017 Crime Stats	Crime and Geographic
Two	HOT SPOTS Montreal Crime Statistics 2015 to 2018	Crime
Three	Montreal Crime Statistics 2015 to 2018	Crime

Operational Lab-Tasks

This map will include geographic and criminal-oriented data, within the large city of Montreal. Concentrations of specific crime and where, are to be explored, throughout various years. An intricate examination of various statistics over a 4-year period is conducted.

Next, the following operational tasks using the capability features of ArcGIS Online will need to be completed, as seen below:

1. Enter Montreal in the right toolbar
2. Left Column Toolbar: Click "Add"
3. See Dropdown Menu: Click "Search for Layers"
4. Type: Montreal Crime
   a. Scroll down, then add the following "Layers":
      1. Montreal PDQ Boundaries Merged with SPVM 2017 Crime Stats
      2. HOT SPOTS Montreal Crime Statistics 2015 to 2018
      3. Montreal Crime Statistics 2015 to 2018
5. If necessary, alter the symbol shape and color for any layer, using "Change Style"
6. Review all relevant data for each layer by clicking "Show Table," prior to formulating and submitting your responses

Once all Layers are added, your map should appear as seen below:

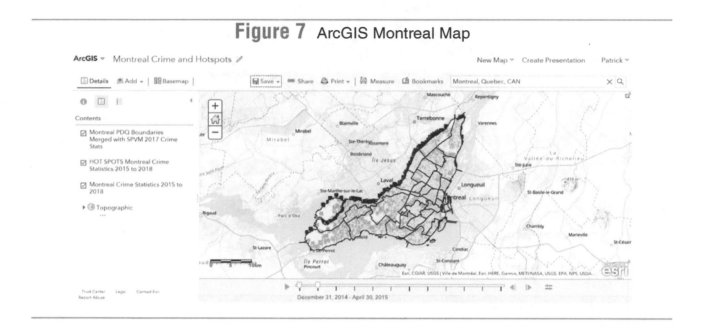

Figure 7 ArcGIS Montreal Map

Part A

Students will respond accordingly to the following questions on this document, using the data provided.

1. In 2017, how many assaults occurred near PDQ-30?
2. In 2017, how many homicides occurred near PDQ-4?
3. In 2017, how many robberies occurred near PDQ-23?
4. In 2017, how many homicides occurred near PDQ-23?
5. In 2017, how many assaults occurred near PDQ-15?
6. In 2017, how many robberies occurred near PDQ-12?
7. In 2017, how many total crimes occurred near PDQ-39?
8. In 2017, how many total crimes occurred near PDQ-7?
9. In 2017, how many total crimes occurred near PDQ-1?
10. In 2017, how many total crimes occurred near PDQ-8?

Part B

Students will now perform an in-depth analysis with the current data in the layers uploaded to create a minimum of ten (10) questions on their own. Responses are only required if the instructor deems necessary:

1. Q1
2. Q2
3. Q3
4. Q4
5. Q5
6. Q6
7. Q7
8. Q8
9. Q9
10. Q10

Lastly, the students will upload this final document into your college's Learning Management System, upon completion.

© krkt/Shutterstock.com

Synopsis of Lab-Theme

Lab Exercise 8 utilizes the state of Texas, and the city of Dallas as the primary jurisdiction. This map contains layers which include data representing a multiyear cross section of crime. Dallas incidents 2017, Dallas incidents 2016, and Dallas incidents 2015 are examined.

© W. Scott McGill/Shutterstock.com

Table 8

Layer #	Layer Name	Data Type
One	Dallas incidents 2017	Crime
Two	Dallas incidents 2016	Crime
Three	Dallas incidents 2015	Crime

Operational Lab-Tasks

This map will include criminal-oriented data, within the city of Dallas. A 3-year exploration of data is comprised of various crimes, ranging in propensity and intensity. Changes may or may not be displayed based on statistics examined.

Next, the following operational tasks using the capability features of ArcGIS Online will need to be completed, as seen below:

1. Enter Dallas in the right toolbar
2. Left Column Toolbar: Click "Add"
3. See Dropdown Menu: Click "Search for Layers"
4. Type: Dallas crime
   a. Scroll down, then add the following "Layers":
      1. Dallas incidents 2017
      2. Dallas incidents 2016
      3. Dallas incidents 2015
5. If necessary, alter the symbol shape and color for any layer, using "Change Style"
6. Review all relevant data for each layer by clicking "Show Table," prior to formulating and submitting your responses

Once all Layers are added, your map should appear as seen below:

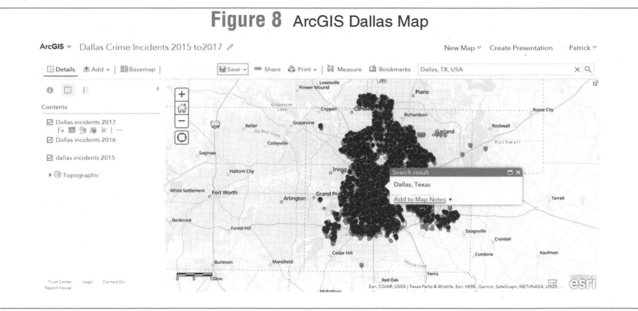

Figure 8 ArcGIS Dallas Map

Part A

Students will respond accordingly to the following questions on this document, using the data provided.

1. How many total incidents occurred in 2015? 4493
2. How many 911 calls reported shootings in 2015? 110
3. How many active shooter-related incidents occurred in 2015? 110
4. How many total incidents occurred in 2017? 5224
5. How many total incidents occurred in 2016? 3838
6. How many burglary-related incidents occurred within 2016? 2146
7. In 2016, how many sudden deaths occurred and documented? 15 accidental unexplained 76 194
8. In 2017, how many incidents involved Road rage? 2
9. In 2015, how many people were reported injured via a 911 telephone call? 64
10. In 2015, how many incidents were reported as a shooting via a 911 telephone call? 110

Part B

Students will now perform an in-depth analysis with the current data in the layers uploaded to create a minimum of ten (10) questions on their own. Responses are only required if the instructor deems necessary:

1. Q1
2. Q2
3. Q3
4. Q4
5. Q5
6. Q6
7. Q7
8. Q8
9. Q9
10. Q10

Lastly, the students will upload this final document into your college's Learning Management System, upon completion.

ArcGIS Online

© life_in_a_pixel/Shutterstock.com

Synopsis of Lab-Theme

Lab Exercise 9 utilizes the state of Tennessee. Lab Exercise 9 aims to also focus on an approach using Strategic Crime Analysis, due to the nature of the type of crimes exhibited in the layers, and on the map, displaying a before and after, temporal-based data set. Tennessee- BeforeCrime and Tennessee-AfterCrime are examined.

© Fer Gregory/Shutterstock.com

Table 9

Layer #	Layer Name	Data-type
One	Tennessee-BeforeCrime	Crime
Two	Tennessee-AfterCrime	Crime

Operational Lab-Tasks

This map will include criminal-oriented data, within the state of Tennessee, as stated. Crimes range in intensity and pattern, highlighted temporal features, based on calendar date and time.

Next, the following operational tasks using the capability features of ArcGIS Online will need to be completed, as seen below:

1. Enter Tennessee in the right toolbar
2. Left Column Toolbar: Click "Add"
3. See Dropdown Menu: Click "Search for Layers"
4. Type: Tennessee crime
   a. Scroll down, then add the following "Layers":
      1. Tennessee-BeforeCrime
      2. Tennessee-AfterCrime
5. If necessary, alter the symbol shape and color for any layer, using "Change Style"
6. Review all relevant data for each layer by clicking "Show Table," prior to formulating and submitting your responses

Once all Layers are added, your map should appear as seen below:

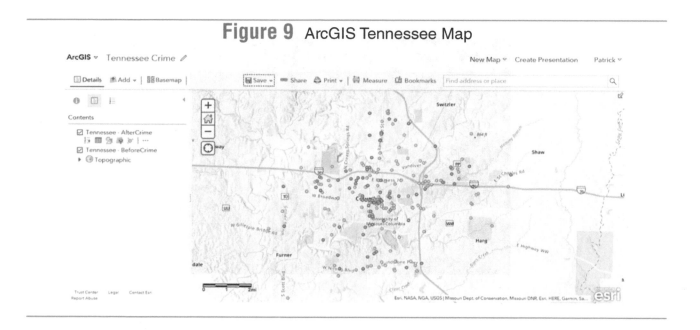

Figure 9 ArcGIS Tennessee Map

Part A

Students will respond accordingly to the following questions on this document, using the data provided.

1. Do all calls possess a timestamp in this layer?
2. How many incidents occurred in Apartment Lot 3?
3. How many people were caught trespassing?
4. How many people were caught harassing others?
5. How many 911 calls were made in 2017?
6. What exactly occurred on Knipp Street?
7. How many times were cops called to assist medics?
8. What exactly occurred on Worley Street?
9. How many people were arrested for a shooting?
10. How many incidents occurred in Apartment Lot 4?

Part B

Students will now perform an in-depth analysis with the current data in the layers uploaded to create a minimum of ten (10) questions on their own. Responses are only required if the instructor deems necessary:

1. Q1
2. Q2
3. Q3
4. Q4
5. Q5
6. Q6
7. Q7
8. Q8
9. Q9
10. Q10

Lastly, the students will upload this final document into your college's Learning Management System, upon completion.

ArcGIS Online

© Branding Pot/Shutterstock.com

Synopsis of Lab-Theme

Lab Exercise 10 utilizes the city of Chicago. Lab Exercise 10 aims to also focus on an approach using Tactical Crime Analysis, due to the nature of the type of crimes exhibited in the layers, and on the map. This city is well known for its violent crimes and death rates due to murder, especially during specific temporal patterns. A multilayer content area is created which includes ranging data also focusing on temporal aspects.

Table 10

Layer #	Layer Name	Data Type
One	Chicago Crime and Facilities Map WFL1-Hospitals	Geographic
Two	Chicago Crime and Facilities Map WFL1-Police Stations	Geographic
Three	Chicago Crime and Facilities Map WFL1-2019 Crime	Crime
Four	Chicago Crime and Facilities Map WFL1-ChicagoCommunities	Geographic
Five	Chicago Crime and Facilities Map WFL1-Census DataPoverty	Geographic
Six	Chicago Crime and Facilities Map WFL1-Crime 2019	Crime

Operational Lab-Tasks

This map will include geographic and criminal-oriented data, within the city of Chicago. Data considerations are displayed which allow for the examination of communities, professional environments and types of crime, and other locations pertinent to crime.

Next, the following operational tasks using the capability features of ArcGIS Online will need to be completed, as seen below:

1. Enter Chicago in the right toolbar
2. Left Column Toolbar: Click "Add"
3. See Dropdown Menu: Click "Search for Layers"
4. Type: Chicago crime
   a. Scroll down, then add the following "Layers":
      1. Chicago Crime and Facilities Map WFL1-Hospitals
      2. Chicago Crime and Facilities Map WFL1-Police Stations
      3. Chicago Crime and Facilities Map WFL1-2019 Crime
      4. Chicago Crime and Facilities Map WFL1-ChicagoCommunities
      5. Chicago Crime and Facilities Map WFL1- CensusDataPoverty
      6. Chicago Crime and Facilities Map WFL1- Crime 2019

5. If necessary, alter the symbol shape and color any layer, using "Change Style"
6. Review all relevant data for each layer by clicking "Show Table," prior to formulating and submitting your responses

Once all Layers are added, your map should appear as seen below:

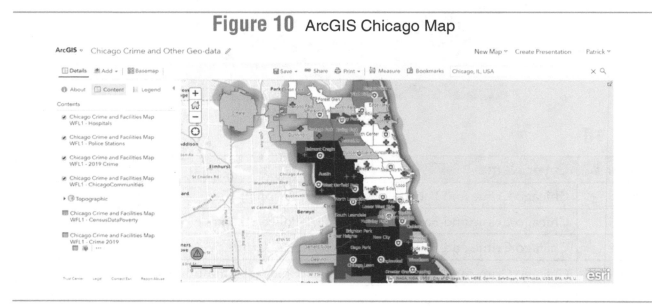

Figure 10 ArcGIS Chicago Map

Part A

Students will respond accordingly to the following questions on this document, using the data provided.

1. How many actual crime incidents exist within this data set?
2. What is the total window of time for which all criminal activity can be accounted for, within this data set?
3. How many different types of locations exist for which crime has occurred?
4. How many primary categories of crime exist within this data set?
5. How many secondary categories of crime exist within this data set?
6. Approximately how many identity thefts over $300.00 exist within this data set?
7. How many deceptive practices occurred within this data set?
8. How many assaults occurred within this data set?
9. How many incidents occurred on a sidewalk within this data set?
10. How many occurrences included a weapons violation?
11. How many police districts are contained in this data set?
12. How many actual police stations exist within this data set?
13. How many hospitals are included within this data set?
14. How many hospitals are considered to be nonprofit?
15. How many hospitals are considered to be federal property?
16. How many total community areas does Chicago possess, per this data set?

17. How many communities possess a household below the poverty line of 40%?
18. How many community areas exist which possess more than 50% of individuals who are 25 years or older without a high school diploma?
19. How many community areas exist which possess less than 50% of individuals who are 25 years or older without a high school diploma?
20. How many community areas exist which possesses over 30% of the people who are over the age of 64?

Part B

Students will now perform an in-depth analysis with the current data in the layers uploaded to create a minimum of ten (10) questions on their own. Responses are only required if the instructor deems necessary:

1. Q1
2. Q2
3. Q3
4. Q4
5. Q5
6. Q6
7. Q7
8. Q8
9. Q9
10. Q10

Lastly, the students will upload this final document into your college's Learning Management System, upon completion.

ArcGIS Online

Synopsis of Lab-Theme

Lab Exercise 11 utilizes the cities of Columbus, Ohio, and Baltimore, Maryland. Lab Exercise 11 aims to focus on an approach using Intelligence Crime Analysis, due to the nature of the type of geographic data, that is, nonhuman surveillance objects, exhibited in the layers, and on the map. Baltimore City Police CCTV Camera locations and Police Crime Cameras—Columbus Crime Camera Location are simultaneously examined.

© ImageFlow/Shutterstock.com

Table 11

Layer #	Layer Name	Data-type
One	Baltimore City Police CCTV Camera Locations	Geographic
Two	Police Crime Cameras—Columbus Crime Camera Location	Geographic

Operational Lab-Tasks

This map will include geographic within the two major American cities. This data represents geographic data which serves as an investigative tool to combat crime, using a spatial analysis.

Next, the following operational tasks using the capability features of ArcGIS Online will need to be completed, as seen below:

1. Enter Columbus, Ohio in the right toolbar, then Baltimore, Maryland in the right toolbar
2. Left Column Toolbar: Click "Add"
3. See Dropdown Menu: Click "Search for Layers"
4. Type: Camera location or police crime cameras
   a. Scroll down, then add the following "Layers":
      1. Baltimore City Police CCTV Camera Locations
      2. Police Crime Cameras—Columbus Crime Camera Location
5. If necessary, alter the symbol shape and color for any layer, using "Change Style"
6. Review all relevant data for each layer by clicking 'Show Table', prior to formulating and submitting your responses

Once all Layers are added, your map should appear as seen below:

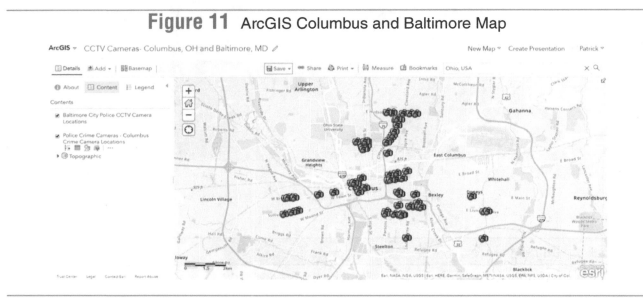

Figure 11 ArcGIS Columbus and Baltimore Map

Part A

Students will respond accordingly to the following questions on this document, using the data provided.

1. How many total camera locations exist in Columbus, Ohio?
2. How many total cameras exist in Baltimore, Maryland?
3. How many total neighborhoods exist within Columbus, Ohio?
4. How many streets, which are also camera locations in Columbus, are observed more than once in this data set?
5. Which neighborhood in Columbus possesses the most camera locations within this data set?
6. Which neighborhood in Columbus possesses the least amount of camera locations within this data set?
7. How many cameras in Columbus possess an identification number over 600?
8. How many cameras in Columbus are downtown?
9. How many cameras in Columbus are considered Far East?
10. How many camera locations may be in an area on a hill?
11. How many camera locations exist in Baltimore?
12. How many camera locations in Baltimore exist near Park Ave?
13. How many camera locations in Baltimore are part of a project that is Downtown?
14. How many camera locations in Baltimore are part of a project that is considered Broadway?
15. How many camera locations in Baltimore are part of a project that is considered Cherry Hill?
16. How many camera locations in Baltimore are part of a project that is considered Greenmount?
17. How many camera locations in Baltimore are part of a project that is considered Monument?

18. How many camera locations in Baltimore are part of a project that is considered Park Heights?
19. How many camera locations in Baltimore are part of a project that is considered Southwest District?
20. How many camera locations in Baltimore are part of a project that is considered Tri-district?
21. How many camera locations in Baltimore are part of a project that is considered Inner Harbor?
22. How many camera locations in Baltimore are part of a project that is considered Nanpond?
23. How many camera locations in Baltimore are part of a project that is considered Federal Reserve?
24. How many camera locations in Baltimore are part of a project that is considered Northeast Market?
25. How many camera locations in Baltimore are part of a project that is considered Hollins Market?
26. How many camera locations in Baltimore are part of a project that is considered McCulloh?
27. How many camera locations in Baltimore are part of a project that is considered Gilmore?
28. How many camera locations in Baltimore are part of a project that is considered Latrobe?
29. How many camera locations in Baltimore are part of a project that is considered Perkins?
30. How many camera locations in Baltimore are part of a project that is considered PVG?

Part B

Students will now perform an in-depth analysis with the current data in the layers uploaded to create a minimum of ten (10) questions on their own. Responses are only required if the instructor deems necessary:

1. Q1
2. Q2
3. Q3
4. Q4
5. Q5
6. Q6
7. Q7
8. Q8
9. Q9
10. Q10

Lastly, the students will upload this final document into your college's Learning Management System, upon completion.

© SevenMaps/Shutterstock.com

Synopsis of Lab-Theme

Lab Exercise 12 utilizes the state of California, and the city of San Bernardino. Lab Exercise 12 aims to also focus on an approach using Tactical Crime Analysis, due to the nature of the type of criminal offender exhibited in the layers, and on the map. Homicides are a focus.

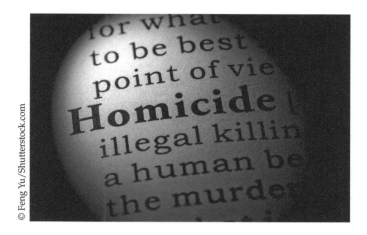

© Feng Yu/Shutterstock.com

Table 12

Layer #	Layer Name	Data Type
One	San Bernardino Homicides 2013	Crime

Operational Lab-Tasks

This map will include criminal-oriented data, within the city of San Bernardino, California. Homicides are profiled during one significant year. This city was also home to one of the most horrific domestic terror events in the last 10 years, if not of all-time.

Next, the following operational tasks using the capability features of ArcGIS Online will need to be completed, as seen below:

1. Enter San Bernardino in the right toolbar
2. Left Column Toolbar: Click "Add"
3. See Dropdown Menu: Click "Search for Layers"
4. Type: San Bernardino crime
   a. Scroll down, then add the following "Layers":
      1. San Bernardino Homicides 2013
5. If necessary, alter the symbol shape and color for this layer, using "Change Style"
6. Review all relevant data for each layer by clicking "Show Table," prior to formulating and submitting your responses;

Once all Layers are added, your map should appear as seen below:

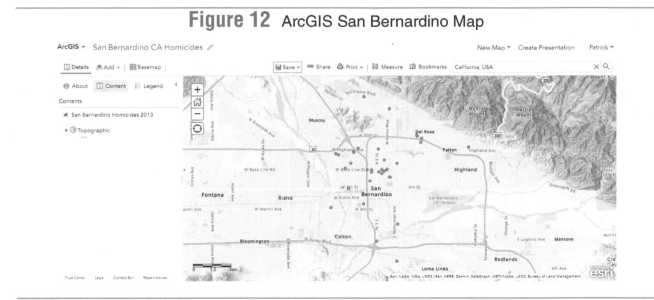

Figure 12 ArcGIS San Bernardino Map

Part A

Students will respond accordingly to the following questions on this document, using the data provided.

1. How many total homicide victims are included in this data set?
2. How many victims were under the age of 20 years old?
3. How many victims were under the age of 30 years old?
4. How many victims were under the age of 40 years old?
5. How many victims were under the age of 50 years old?
6. How many types of injuries exist within this data set?
7. How many times was someone shot within this data set?
8. Which month contained the most homicides within this data set?
9. How many incident numbers include more than one victim?
10. How many different locations of a body exist in this data?

Part B

Students will now perform an in-depth analysis with the current data in the layers uploaded to create a minimum of ten (10) questions on their own. Responses are only required if the instructor deems necessary:

1. Q1
2. Q2
3. Q3
4. Q4
5. Q5
6. Q6
7. Q7
8. Q8
9. Q9
10. Q10

Lastly, the students will upload this final document into your college's Learning Management System, upon completion.

ArcGIS Online

© Greens87/Shutterstock.com

Synopsis of Lab-Theme

Lab Exercise 13 utilizes data which is police-specific, and geographic in nature. All data are represented using content from New Orleans, Louisiana. Administrative Crime Analysis is the precursor, due to the nature of the type of the data exhibited in the layers, and on the map. NOPD Police Subzones/Reporting Districts and NOPD Police Districts are examined.

© Gary Paul Lewis/Shutterstock.com

Table 13

Layer #	Layer Name	Data Type
One	NOPD Police Subzones/Reporting Districts	Geographic
Two	NOPD Police Districts	Geographic

Operational Lab-Tasks

This map will include geographic data from New Orleans, Louisiana. Significant environments are to be examined for spatial analysis, which encompasses a large law enforcement agency.

Next, the following operational tasks using the capability features of ArcGIS Online will need to be completed, as seen below:

1. Enter New Orleans in the right toolbar
2. Left Column Toolbar: Click "Add"
3. See Dropdown Menu: Click "Search for Layers"
4. Type: New Orleans police
   a. Scroll down, then add the following "Layers":
      1. NOPD Police Subzones/Reporting Districts
      2. NOPD Police Districts
5. If necessary, alter the symbol shape and color for any layer, using "Change Style"
6. Review all relevant data for each layer by clicking "Show Table," prior to formulating and submitting your responses

Once all Layers are added, your map should appear as seen below:

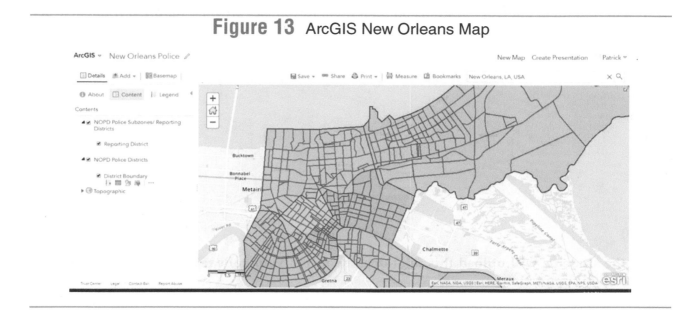

Figure 13 ArcGIS New Orleans Map

Part A

Students will respond accordingly to the following questions on this document, using the data provided.

1. How many total police districts exist within this data set?
2. How many total police subzones exist within this data set?
3. How many zones are located in District 1?
4. How many zones are located in District 8?
5. How many zones are located in District 6?
6. How many zones are located in District 5?
7. How many zones are located in District 7?
8. How many zones are located in District 2?
9. How many zones are located in District 4?
10. How many zones are located in District 3?
11. How many subzones are located in District 8?
12. How many subzones are located in District 5?
13. How many subzones are located in District 1?
14. How many subzones are located in District 3?
15. How many subzones are located in District 7?
16. How many subzones are located in District 4?
17. How many subzones are located in District 2?
18. How many subzones are located in District 6?
19. How many other districts does District 3 border a boundary?
20. How many other districts does District 5 border a boundary?

Part B

Students will now perform an in-depth analysis with the current data in the layers uploaded to create a minimum of ten (10) questions on their own. Responses are only required if the instructor deems necessary:

1. Q1
2. Q2
3. Q3
4. Q4
5. Q5
6. Q6
7. Q7
8. Q8
9. Q9
10. Q10

Lastly, the students will upload this final document into your college's Learning Management System, upon completion.

ArcGIS Online

Synopsis of Lab-Theme

Lab Exercise 14 utilizes the state of North Carolina. Lab Exercise 14 aims to focus on an approach using Administrative Crime Analysis, due to the nature of the type of geographic data exhibited in the layer, and on the map. Correctional Institutions are the focus.

Table 14

Layer #	Layer Name	Data Type
One	Correctional Institutions	Geographic

Operational Lab-Tasks

This map will include geographic data, within the state of North Carolina, as stated. Also, spatial analysis is the key factor as law enforcement agencies are the focal point.

Next, the following operational tasks using the capability features of ArcGIS Online will need to be completed, as seen below:

1. Enter North Carolina in the right toolbar
2. Left Column Toolbar: Click "Add"
3. See Dropdown Menu: Click "Search for Layers"
4. Type: North Carolina crime
   a. Scroll down, then add the following "Layers":
      1. Correctional Institutions
5. If necessary, alter the symbol shape and color for this layer, using "Change Style"
6. Review all relevant data for each layer by clicking "Show Table," prior to formulating and submitting your responses

Once all Layers are added, your map should appear as seen below:

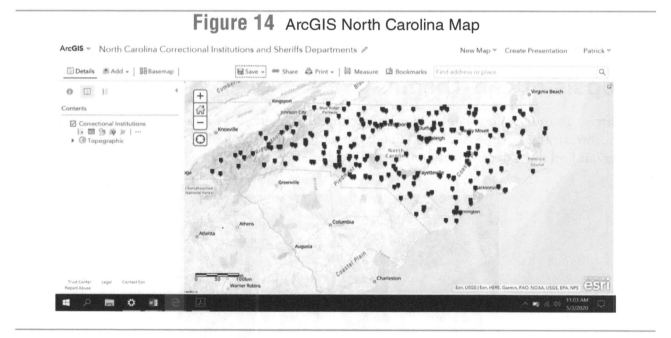

Figure 14 ArcGIS North Carolina Map

Part A

Students will respond accordingly to the following questions on this document, using the data provided.

1. Does Transylvania contain Female inmates?
2. Which Federal institutions are exhibited within this data?
3. How many County jails exist within this data?
4. How many jails house Juvenile Offenders from this data set?
5. How many Counties are represented in this data set?
6. Whose driveway entrance is located on the westside of State Highway 251 North?
7. How many "residential" facilities exist within this data set?
8. How many prisons are documented within this data set?
9. What institution is located on the North side of Old Highway 75?
10. What is Southwest of Hagan Street?
11. What is located on the Southeast side of Coliseum Drive?
12. How many institutions are located in Cumberland County?
13. How many counties possess a county jail?
14. How many institutions are located in Craven?
15. How many counties possess a juvenile detention center?

Part B

Students will now perform an in-depth analysis with the current data in the layers uploaded to create a minimum of ten (10) questions on their own. Responses are only required if the instructor deems necessary:

1. Q1
2. Q2
3. Q3
4. Q4
5. Q5
6. Q6
7. Q7
8. Q8
9. Q9
10. Q10

Lastly, the students will upload this final document into your college's Learning Management System, upon completion.

MARYLAND_EPS 10 VECTOR MAP

© tunasalmon/Shutterstock.com

Synopsis of Lab-Theme

Lab Exercise 15 utilizes the state of Maryland, as the primary jurisdiction. This map contains layers which include data representing police data which is geographic in nature. It also demonstrates a multijurisdictional approach for agencies, which examines Administrative Crime Analysis. Maryland Police-Federal Police Stations, Maryland Police-Municipal Police Stations, Maryland Police-University Police Stations, Maryland Police-County Police Stations, Maryland Police-State Police Stations, and Maryland Police-Other Police Stations are examined.

Table 15

Layer #	Layer Name	Data Type
One	Maryland Police-Federal Police Stations	Geographic
Two	Maryland Police-Municipal Police Stations	Geographic
Three	Maryland Police-University Police Stations	Geographic
Four	Maryland Police-County Police Stations	Geographic
Five	Maryland Police-State Police Stations	Geographic
Six	Maryland Police-Other Police Stations	Geographic

Operational Lab-Tasks

This map will include geographic data, within the state of Maryland, as stated. Various police agencies comprise the geographic data, yet also maintains the aim to also acknowledge spatial analysis.

Next, the following operational tasks using the capability features of ArcGIS Online will need to be completed, as seen below:

1. Enter Maryland in the right toolbar
2. Left Column Toolbar: Click "Add"
3. See Dropdown Menu: Click "Search for Layers"
4. Type: Maryland police
    a. Scroll down, then add the following "Layers":
        1. Maryland Police-Federal Police Stations
        2. Maryland Police-Municipal Police Stations
        3. Maryland Police-University Police Stations
        4. Maryland Police-County Police Stations
        5. Maryland Police-State Police Stations
        6. Maryland Police-Other Police Stations

5. If necessary, alter the symbol shape and color for any layer, using "Change Style"
6. Review all relevant data for each layer by clicking "Show Table," prior to formulating and sub-mitting your responses

Once all Layers are added, your map should appear as seen below:

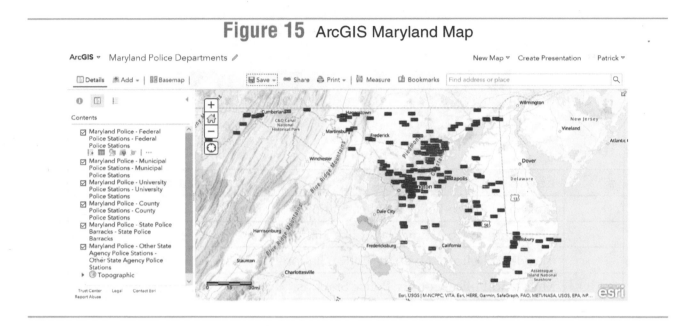

Figure 15 ArcGIS Maryland Map

Part A

Students will respond accordingly to the following questions on this document, using the data provided.

1. How many police agencies are located in Frederick County?
2. How many University Police stations are located in Baltimore City?
3. How many Federal Police Stations are within this data set?
4. What county is the Metropolitan Transportation Authority Police located?
5. What county is the Maryland Aviation Administration located?
6. How many University Police stations are located in Baltimore County?
7. Which Federal Police station is located in Anne Arundel?
8. Calvert County is home to what Barrack?
9. What county is Headquarters located?
10. What is the distance in miles, from Barrack S to Barrack B?

Part B

Students will now perform an in-depth analysis with the current data in the layers uploaded to create a minimum of ten (10) questions on their own. Responses are only required if the instructor deems necessary:

1. Q1
2. Q2
3. Q3
4. Q4
5. Q5
6. Q6
7. Q7
8. Q8
9. Q9
10. Q10

Lastly, the students will upload this final document into your college's Learning Management System, upon completion.

ArcGIS Online

© Rudy Balasko/Shutterstock.com

Synopsis of Lab-Theme

Lab Exercise 16 utilizes the city of St. Louis, Missouri, as the primary jurisdiction. This map contains layers which include data representing crime, and crime hotspots, in one of the most active cities in America. Lab Exercise 16 aims to also focus on an approach using Strategic Crime Analysis, due to the nature of the type of crime exhibited in the layers, and on the map, especially the clusters and density. Hot Spots St. Louis Crime KKE and St. Louis Crime KKE are examined.

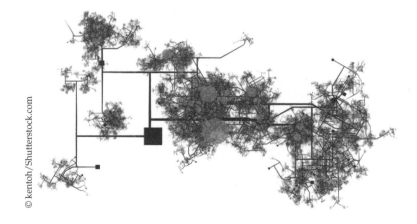

© kentoh/Shutterstock.com

Table 16

Layer #	Layer Name	Data Type
One	Hot Spots St. Louis Crime KKE	Crime
Two	St. Louis Crime KKE	Crime

Operational Lab-Tasks

This map will include criminal-oriented data, within the city of St. Louis, as stated. Crime hotspots, using various types of crimes as data, are examined. Temporal and spatial analysis are incorporated.

Next, the following operational tasks using the capability features of ArcGIS Online will need to be completed, as seen below:

1. Enter St. Louis in the right toolbar
2. Left Column Toolbar: Click "Add"
3. See Dropdown Menu: Click "Search for Layers"
4. Type: St. Louis crime
   a. Scroll down, then add the following "Layers":
      1. Hot Spots St. Louis Crime KKE
      2. St. Louis Crime KKE
5. If necessary, alter the symbol shape and color for any layer, using "Change Style"
6. Review all relevant data for each layer by clicking "Show Table," prior to formulating and submitting your responses

Once all Layers are added, your map should appear as seen below:

Figure 16 ArcGIS St. Louis Map

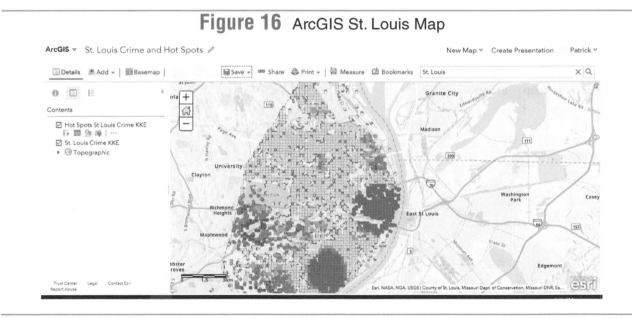

Part A

Students will respond accordingly to the following questions on this document, using the data provided.

1. How many hotspots are considered to be significant?
2. Which numbered hotspot possessed the highest amount of crime incidents?
3. How many hotspots are considered to be not significant?
4. How many coldspots are displayed in this data set?
5. How many number of points of the same amount are within this data set?
6. How many crime complaints are there within St. Louis in this data?
7. What is the total amount of years which this data set accounts for?
8. Which district possessed the most crime in this data set?
9. How many people with arrested for stealing by deceit?
10. Which neighborhood is Arthur Avenue within?

Part B

Students will now perform an in-depth analysis with the current data in the layers uploaded to create a minimum of ten (10) questions on their own. Responses are only required if the instructor deems necessary:

1. Q1
2. Q2
3. Q3
4. Q4
5. Q5
6. Q6
7. Q7
8. Q8
9. Q9
10. Q10

Lastly, the students will upload this final document into your college's Learning Management System, upon completion.

© Andrija Markovic/Shutterstock.com

Synopsis of Lab-Theme

Lab Exercise 17 utilizes the entire globe, or major parts of many continents, as the primary jurisdiction. This map contains a layer which includes data representing terror over time, across the world. Intelligence Crime Analysis is the focus as well, due to the nature of the type of crimes, and the data which are exhibited on the map. Global Terrorism Database is examined.

© santoelia/Shutterstock.com

Table 17

Layer #	Layer Name	Data Type
One	Global Terrorism Database	Crime

Operational Lab-Tasks

This map will include criminal-oriented data, using global approach, considering the war on terror, past and present. Spatial analysis highlights the criminality and the perpetrators' commission, while temporal analysis is required to encompass the regions.

Next, the following operational tasks using the capability features of ArcGIS Online will need to be completed, as seen below:

1. Enter any continent in the right toolbar
2. Left Column Toolbar: Click "Add"
3. See Dropdown Menu: Click "Search for Layers"
4. Type: Terror
   a. Scroll down, then add the following "Layers":
      1. Global Terrorism Database
5. If necessary, alter the symbol shape and color for this layer, using "Change Style"
6. Review all relevant data for each layer by clicking "Show Table," prior to formulating and submitting your responses

Once all Layers are added, your map should appear as seen below:

Figure 17 ArcGIS Global Terror Map

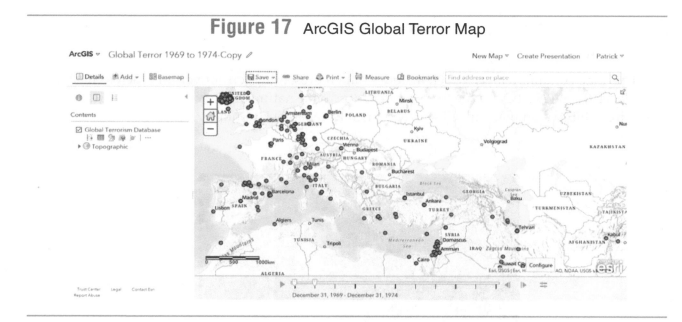

Part A

Students will respond accordingly to the following questions on this document, using the data provided.

1. How many terror incidents occurred in Southeast Asia from 1969 to 1974?
2. How many incidents occurred outside an embassy?
3. How many kidnappings occurred within this data set?
4. How many private citizens were targeted within this data set?
5. Who were responsible for any and all incidents considered to be a Melee?
6. Who is Janjaweed?
7. Who may have committed terror acts in Cyprus?
8. What occurred in East Timor?
9. How many banks in Colombia were targeted?
10. Where is Ain Defla?
11. How many countries were victims of a terror incident?
12. How many times was Mexico a location for terror?
13. How many assassinations occurred within this data set?
14. How many times were the Military a target for terror?
15. How many embassies were targeted in relation to terror?
16. How many times was electricity targeted in relation to terror?
17. How many times was the New Year's Gang?
18. How many incidents involved Incendiary devices?
19. How many armed assaults targeted police?
20. What occurred in Jersey City, New Jersey?

Part B

Students will now perform an in-depth analysis with the current data in the layers uploaded to create a minimum of ten (10) questions on their own. Responses are only required if the instructor deems necessary:

1. Q1
2. Q2
3. Q3
4. Q4
5. Q5
6. Q6
7. Q7
8. Q8
9. Q9
10. Q10

Lastly, the students will upload this final document into your college's Learning Management System, upon completion.

ArcGIS Online

© Kursat Unsal/Shutterstock.com

Synopsis of Lab-Theme

Lab Exercise 18 utilizes the city of Kansas City, Missouri, as the primary jurisdiction. This map contains layers which include data representing police geographic data necessary for spatial analysis. Lab Exercise 18 aims to also focus on an approach using Administrative Crime Analysis, due to the nature of the type of data exhibited in the layers, and on the map. Kansas City Districts and Divisions, as well as Kansas City MO Police Stations, are examined.

© Tana888/Shutterstock.com

Table 18

Layer #	Layer Name	Data Type
One	Kansas City Districts and Divisions	Geographic
Two	Kansas City MO Police Stations	Geographic

Operational Lab-Tasks

This map will include geographic data within the city of Kansas City, Missouri. Spatial analysis is utilized to explore all vital geographic variables for law enforcement agencies.

Next, the following operational tasks using the capability features of ArcGIS Online will need to be completed, as seen below:

1. Enter Kansas City in the right toolbar
2. Left Column Toolbar: Click "Add"
3. See Dropdown Menu: Click "Search for Layers"
4. Type: Kansas City police
   a. Scroll down, then add the following "Layers":
      1. Kansas City Districts and Divisions
      2. Kansas City MO Police Stations
5. If necessary, alter the symbol shape and color for any layer, using "Change Style"
6. Review all relevant data for each layer by clicking "Show Table," prior to formulating and submitting your responses

Once all Layers are added, your map should appear as seen below:

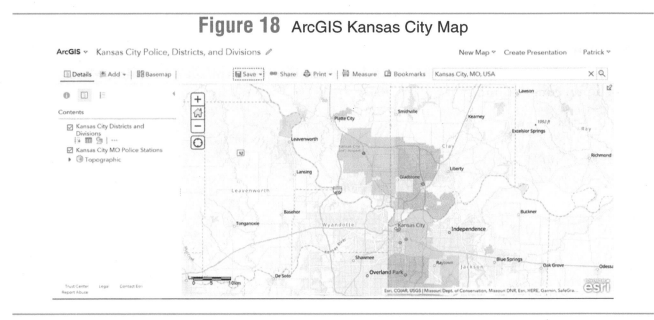

Figure 18 ArcGIS Kansas City Map

Part A

Students will respond accordingly to the following questions on this document, using the data provided.

1. How many districts are located in Division 3?
2. How many districts are located in Division 6?
3. How many districts are located in Division 1?
4. How many districts are located in Division 2?
5. How many districts are located in Division 4?
6. How many districts are located in Division 5?
7. How many sectors are located in Division 2?
8. How many sectors are located in Division 1?
9. How many sectors are located in Division 3?
10. How many sectors are located in Division 4?

Part B

Students will now perform an in-depth analysis with the current data in the layers uploaded to create a minimum of ten (10) questions on their own. Responses are only required if the instructor deems necessary:

1. Q1
2. Q2
3. Q3
4. Q4
5. Q5
6. Q6
7. Q7
8. Q8
9. Q9
10. Q10

Lastly, the students will upload this final document into your college's Learning Management System, upon completion.

Synopsis of Lab-Theme

Lab Exercise 19 utilizes the city of Milwaukee, as the primary jurisdiction. This map contains layers which include data representing various years of crime incidents. Lab Exercise 19 aims to also focus on an approach using Strategic Crime Analysis, due to the nature of the type of criminal activity exhibited in the layers, and on the map. Layers will include 2016 Crime Data, 2017 Crime Data, 2018 Crime Data, to be examined.

Table 19

Layer #	Layer Name	Data Type
One	2016 Crime Data	Crime
Two	2017 Crime Data	Crime
Three	2018 Crime Data	Crime

Operational Lab-Tasks

This map will include criminal-oriented data, within the city of Milwaukee. A 3-year cross section is explored for temporal analysis.

Next, the following operational tasks using the capability features of ArcGIS Online will need to be completed, as seen below:

1. Enter Milwaukee in the right toolbar
2. Left Column Toolbar: Click "Add"
3. See Dropdown Menu: Click "'Search for Layers"
4. Type: Milwaukee crime
    a. Scroll down, then add the following "Layers":
        1. 2016 Crime Data
        2. 2017 Crime Data
        3. 2018 Crime Data
5. If necessary, alter the symbol shape and color any layer, using "Change Style"
6. Review all relevant data for each layer by clicking "Show Table," prior to formulating and submitting your responses

Once all Layers are added, your map should appear as seen below:

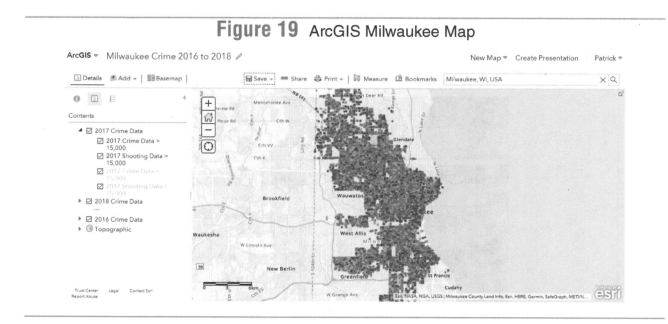

Figure 19 ArcGIS Milwaukee Map

Part A

Students will respond accordingly to the following questions on this document, using the data provided.

1. In 2017, how many times was a gun used as a weapon?
2. In 2017, how many times was a motor vehicle used as a weapon?
3. In 2017, how many times were a suspects' hands considered as a weapon during a crime?
4. How many times did a crime occur on 7th street in 2017?
5. What occurred on Roosevelt Drive in 207?
6. How many wards were locations for burglaries?
7. In 2017, how many crime incidents involved a locked vehicle?
8. In 2017, how many crimes with shooting data were cleared by arrest?
9. How many times in 2017 was an Assignment Completed relevant to shooting data?
10. In 2017, did a shooting occur in Ward 267?

Part B

Students will now perform an in-depth analysis with the current data in the layers uploaded to create a minimum of ten (10) questions on their own. Responses are only required if the instructor deems necessary:

1. Q1
2. Q2
3. Q3
4. Q4
5. Q5
6. Q6
7. Q7
8. Q8
9. Q9
10. Q10

Lastly, the students will upload this final document into your college's Learning Management System, upon completion.

ArcGIS Online

© Marcio Jose Bastos Silva/Shutterstock.com

Synopsis of Lab-Theme

Lab Exercise 20 utilizes crime data from the Middle East, spawned from the criminal activity, and data, propelled by a major security threat group. Lab Exercise 20 aims to also focus on an approach using Intelligence Crime Analysis, due to the nature of the type of criminal activity exhibited in the layers, and on the map. ISIS Attacks 2014, ISIS Attacks 2015 Part 1, and ISIS Attacks 2015 Part 2 are examined.

Table 20

Layer #	Layer Name	Data Type
One	ISIS Attacks 2014	Crime
Two	ISIS Attacks 2015 Part 1	Crime
Three	ISIS Attacks 2015 Part 2	Crime

Operational Lab-Tasks

This map will include criminal-oriented data, within a specific jurisdiction across the globe, focusing on terror incidents sparks by ISIS. Multiple years are explored, as some deviation may or may not be present pertinent to temporal analysis.

Next, the following operational tasks using the capability features of ArcGIS Online will need to be completed, as seen below:

1. Enter Middle East in the right toolbar
2. Left Column Toolbar: Click "Add"
3. See Dropdown Menu: Click "Search for Layers"
4. Type: ISIS or terror
    a. Scroll down, then add the following "Layers":
        1. ISIS Attacks 2014
        2. ISIS Attacks 2015 Part 1
        3. ISIS Attacks 2015 Part 2
5. If necessary, alter the symbol shape and color for any layer, using "Change Style"
6. Review all relevant data for each layer by clicking "Show Table," prior to formulating and submitting your responses

Once all Layers are added, your map should appear as seen below:

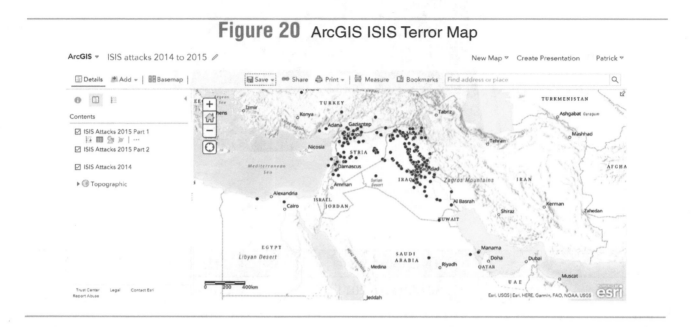

Figure 20 ArcGIS ISIS Terror Map

Part A

Students will respond accordingly to the following questions on this document, using the data provided.

1. How many times in 2014 did ISIS commit an attack?
2. How many times in 2014 did ISIS commit an attack in Aleppo?
3. How many miles away is Shakur from Shirqat?
4. How many attacks occur in Oman in 2014?
5. How many attacks occurred in Syria in 2014?
6. How many attacks occurred in 2014 in Egypt?
7. How many attacks occurred in 2014 in Iran?
8. In 2015, how many times did ISIS perform an attack in Turkey?
9. In 2015, how many times did ISIS perform an attack in Lebanon?
10. In 2015, how many times did ISIS perform an attack in Syria?
11. In 2015, how many times did ISIS perform an attack in Iraq?
12. In 2015, how many times did ISIS perform an attack in Iran?
13. In 2015, how many times did ISIS perform an attack in Saudi Arabia?
14. In 2015, how many times did ISIS perform an attack in Paris?
15. In 2015, how many times did ISIS perform an attack in Zummar?
16. In 2015, how many times did ISIS perform an attack in Tripoli?
17. In 2015, how many times did ISIS perform an attack in Tunisia?
18. In 2015, how many times did ISIS perform an attack in Shawuk?
19. In 2015, how many times did ISIS perform an attack in Tall Ar Rim?
20. In 2015, how many times did ISIS perform an attack in Sinjar?

Part B

Students will now perform an in-depth analysis with the current data in the layers uploaded to create a minimum of ten (10) questions on their own. Responses are only required if the instructor deems necessary:

1. Q1
2. Q2
3. Q3
4. Q4
5. Q5
6. Q6
7. Q7
8. Q8
9. Q9
10. Q10

Lastly, the students will upload this final document into your college's Learning Management System, upon completion.

SECTION 2

Applied Learning Framework for 'Rate' Typology—Crime Rate

Using "Rates," in conjunction with performing mathematical modeling, allows for the translation of tell-tale analyses that allow multiple audiences to understand the significance of occurring crime in jurisdictions committed throughout the United States, as well as the rest of the world. Law enforcement agencies possess a vital need to present and communicate timely and accurate data retrieval for the dissemination of findings. Usually this data is verbally transferred from an agency to its employees, or an agency to a community. Crime rates are indicators of reported crime activity standardized by population.

A multitude of other purposes are served through these processes of establishing "Rates," such as: investigatory matters, assessing the performance of police, budget allowances and resource allocation, and the evaluation of crime analysis and experimental programs. All of these components assist in the combat, prevention, deterrence, and overall attempts to control crime.

Quick Procedural Practice

A crime rate is defined as the number of crime offenses per every 100,000 humans within a jurisdiction, or its population. The crime rate is formulated by first dividing a jurisdiction's actual population by 100,000, and then dividing the number of offenses by the result. Crime rates are disseminated from law enforcement agencies for which 12 months, or once calendar year of complete reported data, has been submitted.

One example is observing a population for a jurisdiction, which in this case will be 75,000. Next a number of known crimes for this jurisdiction, within 1 year, is 215 crimes. Upon receiving the task of configuring a Crime Rate, the operator can then divide 75,000 by 100,000, which will produce a figure of 0.75. Next, the user will divide 215 crimes by 0.75, hence creating the additional figure of 286.7. This figure can then be communicated and documented as a "crime rate" of 286.7 per 100,000 inhabitants.

The number 0.75 can now be divided into the totals of any offense category to produce a crime rate for that specific offense.

ArcGIS Online

© Casimiro PT/Shutterstock.com

Synopsis of Lab-Theme

Lab Exercise 21 utilizes the United States of America, whereas data display a significant type of criminal, over time. Lab Exercise 21 aims to also focus on an approach using Strategic Crime Analysis, due to the nature of the type of criminal offender exhibited in the layers, and on the map. Serial Killers-Characteristics of perpetrator, Serial Killers-Food Targeted, Serial Killers-Victims, and Serial Killers-where are examined.

© breakermaximus/Shutterstock.com

Table 21

Layer #	Layer Name	Data Type
One	Serial Killers-Characteristics of perpetrator	Crime
Two	Serial Killers-Food Targeted	Crime
Three	Serial Killers-Victims	Crime and Geographic
Four	Serial Killers-where	Geographic

Operational Lab-Tasks

This map will include geographic and criminal-oriented data, within our nation, examining temporal and spatial data as correlated with violent offenders, specifically Serial Killers. Also, various modes of attack on victims are examined.

Next, the following operational tasks using the capability features of ArcGIS Online will need to be completed, as seen below:

1. Enter USA in the right toolbar
2. Left Column Toolbar: Click "Add"
3. See Dropdown Menu: Click "Search for Layers"
4. Type: Serial Killers
   a. Scroll down, then add the following "Layers":
      1. Sex Serial Killers-Characteristics of perpetrator
      2. Serial Killers-Food Targeted
      3. Serial Killers-Victims
      4. Serial Killers-where
5. If necessary, alter the symbol shape and color for any layer, using "Change Style"
6. Review all relevant data for each layer by clicking "Show Table," prior to formulating and submitting your responses

Once all Layers are added, your map should appear as seen below:

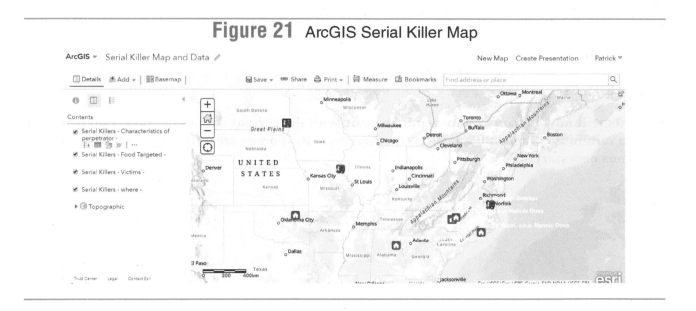

Figure 21 ArcGIS Serial Killer Map

Part A

Students will respond accordingly to the following questions on this document, using the data provided.

1. What is the total amount of years that these layers cover, based on the data provided?
2. How many countries are included as locations for incidents which have occurred?
3. How many incidents targeted a victims' drink(s) to cause harm?
4. How many perpetrators were Female?
5. How many perpetrators were Housewives?
6. How many targets of a perpetrator were considered a Friend?
7. What type of punishment did Mattia Del Zotto receive for his actions?
8. How many people died due to all of these incidents?
9. How many victims were injured due to these incidents?
10. How many Agents may have been created at the location of where the perpetrator lives?
11. How many total cities comprise the specific jurisdictions of these incidents?
12. How many health facilities were used as locations to commit a crime?
13. Who used some form of Salmonella to cause harm during an incident?
14. How many perpetrators may have been employed while committing crimes within this dataset?
15. Which Serial Killer possesses the most homicides in this data set?
16. How often did Michael Swango commit crimes?
17. How many perpetrators may have been a Nannie?
18. How many total "Serial Killers" comprise this data set?
19. Who may have used the chemical Ricin to cause harm?
20. How many times did Europe become a victim to a Serial Killer, as per this data?

21. Which Serial Killer injured the most people?
22. How many times was the United States a victim to a Serial Killer, per this data?
23. How many perpetrators may have been Japanese?
24. How many perpetrators were from Canada?
25. Who ate cake?

Part B

Students will now perform an in-depth analysis with the current data in the layers uploaded to create a minimum of ten (10) questions on their own. Responses are only required if the instructor deems necessary:

1. Q1
2. Q2
3. Q3
4. Q4
5. Q5
6. Q6
7. Q7
8. Q8
9. Q9
10. Q10

Part C

Crime Rate Calculations

Serial Killer Murders: 4155
Population: 45,765,889
Crime Rate =

Lastly, the students will upload this final document into your college's Learning Management System, upon completion.

© Kursat Unsal/Shutterstock.com

Synopsis of Lab-Theme

Lab Exercise 22 utilizes the city of Boston, as the primary jurisdiction. This map contains layers which include data representing geographic and crime activity, including schools. Lab Exercise 22 aims to also focus on an approach using Tactical Crime Analysis, due to the nature of the type of crimes and other locations exhibited in the layers, and on the map. School to Police, School to Police—Connecting Lines, and Minn 2017 Crime Boston are examined.

© 4kclips/Shutterstock.com

Table 22

Layer #	Layer Name	Data Type
One	School to Police	Geographic
Two	School to Police—Connecting Lines	Geographic
Three	Minn 2017 Crime Boston	Crime

Operational Lab-Tasks

This map will include geographic and criminal-oriented data, within the city of Boston, as stated. Also, schools and police stations within a specific distance are utilized to focus on proximity.

Next, the following operational tasks using the capability features of ArcGIS Online will need to be completed, as seen below:

1. Enter Boston in the right toolbar
2. Left Column Toolbar: Click "Add"
3. See Dropdown Menu: Click "Search for Layers"
4. Type: Boston police
   a. Scroll down, then add the following "Layers":
      1. School to Police
      2. School to Police—Connecting Lines
      3. Minn 2017 Crime Boston
5. If necessary, alter the symbol shape and color for any layer, using "Change Style"
6. Review all relevant data for each layer by clicking "Show Table," prior to formulating and submitting your responses

Once all Layers are added, your map should appear as seen below:

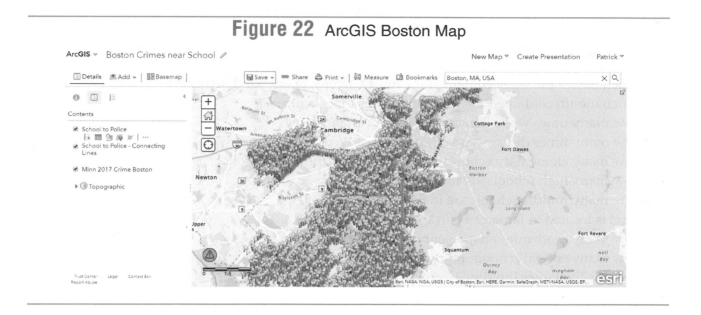

Figure 22 ArcGIS Boston Map

Part A

Students will respond accordingly to the following questions on this document, using the data provided.

1. How many total auto thefts occurred within the timeframe displayed?
2. How many aggravated assaults occurred within the timeframe displayed?
3. How many warrant arrests occurred within this data set?
4. How many verbal disputes occurred within this data set?
5. How many times did someone threaten another with bodily harm?
6. How many times was a witness intimidated?
7. Did anyone use burglary tools to break the law?
8. How much crime involved trespassing on another's property?
9. Which district was the busiest in Boston?
10. How many reporting areas does C6 possess?
11. How many districts included "0" crime whatsoever?
12. Which day of the week contained the most crime to occur?
13. Which month contained the most crime that occurred?
14. How many times was a Landlord involved in an incident?
15. How many times did a Vandalism occur on a Friday?
16. How many total thefts occurred within the timeframe displayed?
17. How many restraining orders were in place in this time frame?
18. How many warrant arrests occurred on a Tuesday?
19. How many verbal disputes occurred on a weekend day?
20. How many times did someone inflict bodily harm?

21. How many times was suicide attempted?
22. Did anyone use an Ax to break the law?
23. How much crime involved destruction of another's property?
24. Which district was the second-busiest in Boston?
25. How many reporting areas does E13 possess?
26. How many districts included "2" to "5" crimes?
27. Which day of the week contained the most Larceny, of any kind, to occur?
28. Which month contained the most homicides that occurred?
29. How many times was a Tenant involved in an incident?
30. How many times did any Assault occur on a Wednesday?
31. How many elementary schools are in distance to the Boston Police?
32. How many high schools are in Roxbury?
33. How many middle schools are in South Boston?
34. What is located in Jamaica Plain?
35. How many academies are present in this data set?
36. How many special schools are present in this data set?
37. Where is the Fuller Building?
38. How many buildings may have been named after U.S. Presidents?
39. How far away is Dorchester Academy from Madison Park?
40. Which school possesses the shortest distance to a police station, per this data set?
41. How police departments are less than a quarter-mile from a school?
42. How many police departments are on Washington Street?
43. How many police departments are over two (2) stories, in height?
44. How many schools are in Mattapan?
45. How many schools are under a half-mile from a police station?

Part B

Students will now perform an in-depth analysis with the current data in the layers uploaded to create a minimum of ten (10) questions on their own. Responses are only required if the instructor deems necessary:

1. Q1
2. Q2
3. Q3
4. Q4
5. Q5
6. Q6
7. Q7
8. Q8
9. Q9
10. Q10

Lastly, the students will upload this final document into your college's Learning Management System, upon completion.

ArcGIS Online

© Wangkun Jia/Shutterstock.com

Synopsis of Lab-Theme

Lab Exercise 23 utilizes Canada, and its leading law enforcement agency. Lab Exercise 23 aims to also focus on an approach using Strategic Crime Analysis, due to the nature of the type of crime exhibited in the layers, and on the map. Missing People of Canada and RCMP Detachments are examined.

© Imfoto/Shutterstock.com

Table 23

Layer #	Layer Name	Data Type
One	Missing People of Canada	Crime and Geographic
Two	RCMP Detachments	Geographic

Operational Lab-Tasks

This map will include geographic and criminal-oriented data, within Canada. Missing persons comprise crime data, while the Royal Canadian Mounted Police represent the geocoding. Spatial analysis and the proximity of crime is a focal point.

Next, the following operational tasks using the capability features of ArcGIS Online will need to be completed, as seen below:

1. Enter Canada in the right toolbar
2. Left Column Toolbar: Click "Add"
3. See Dropdown Menu: Click "Search for Layers"
4. Type: RCMP
   a. Scroll down, then add the following "Layers":
      1. Missing People of Canada
      2. RCMP Detachments
5. If necessary, alter the symbol shape and color for any layer, using "Change Style"
6. Review all relevant data for each layer by clicking "Show Table," prior to formulating and submitting your responses

Once all Layers are added, your map should appear as seen below:

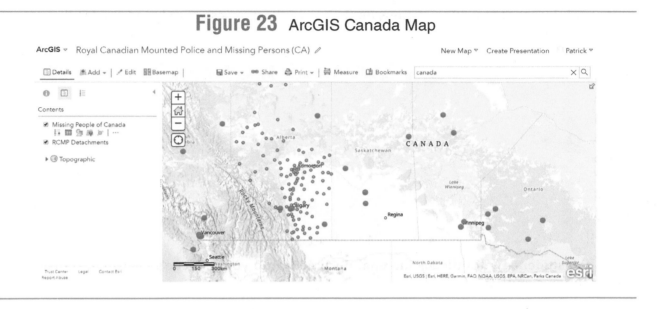

Figure 23 ArcGIS Canada Map

Part A

Students will respond accordingly to the following questions on this document, using the data provided.

1. How many total detachments for the RCMP are in this data set?
2. How many Canadian provinces are located in this data set?
3. How many detachments may include being located on a hill?
4. How many detachments may be located near a river?
5. How many detachments may be near a lake?
6. How many people over the age of 50, are missing?
7. Which decade displays the most persons to have gone missing?
8. How many people named Murdo, may actually be murdered?
9. Who was the youngest person to have went missing?
10. Which detachment is Linda Airut closest to?

Part B

Students will now perform an in-depth analysis with the current data in the layers uploaded to create a minimum of ten (10) questions on their own. Responses are only required if the instructor deems necessary:

1. Q1
2. Q2
3. Q3
4. Q4
5. Q5
6. Q6
7. Q7
8. Q8
9. Q9
10. Q10

Lastly, the students will upload this final document into your college's Learning Management System, upon completion.

© Vector FX/Shutterstock.com

Synopsis of Lab-Theme

Lab Exercise 24 utilizes the United States. This map contains crimes which include data representing domestic terrorism. Lab Exercise 24 aims to also focus on an approach using Intelligence Crime Analysis, due to the nature of the 15-year window exhibited in the layers, and on the map. Violent Extremists Attacks 2001 to 2016 is examined.

© alexkich/Shutterstock.com

Table 24

Layer #	Layer Name	Data Type
One	Violent Extremists Attacks 2001 to 2016	Crime and Geographic

Operational Lab-Tasks

This map will include geographic and criminal-oriented data, within the USA, focusing on domestic terror, as stated. Temporal and spatial analysis is ever present, and its foundations begin on 2001 to 2016.

Next, the following operational tasks using the capability features of ArcGIS Online will need to be completed, as seen below:

1. Enter USA in the right toolbar
2. Left Column Toolbar: Click "Add"
3. See Dropdown Menu: Click "Search for Layers"
4. Type: Terror
   a. Scroll down, then add the following "Layers":
      1. Violent Extremists Attacks 2001 to 2016
5. If necessary, alter the symbol shape and color for this layer, using "Change Style";
6. Review all relevant data for each layer by clicking "Show Table," prior to formulating and submitting your responses;

Once all Layers are added, your map should appear as seen below:

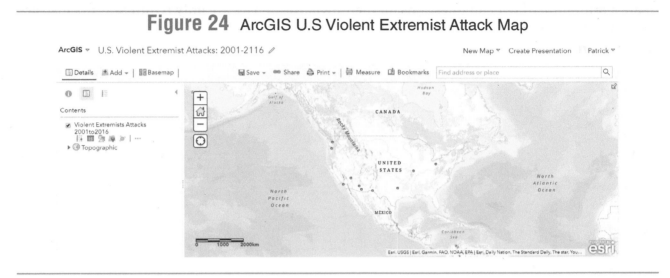

Figure 24 ArcGIS U.S Violent Extremist Attack Map

Part A

Students will respond accordingly to the following questions on this document, using the data provided.

1. How many attacks occurred in Mays Landing?
2. How many extremist groups are considered Far Right?
3. Which incident occurred on Long Island, New York?
4. How many incidents were triggered by a White Supremacist?
5. How many incidents occurred in Oregon?
6. Did any of these events occur inside a museum?
7. Who was involved in the incident where a child molester was involved?
8. How many incidents included more than one perpetrator?
9. Which year included the most incidents of this kind?
10. Which month possessed the most incidents to occur in this data set?

Part B

Students will now perform an in-depth analysis with the current data in the layers uploaded to create a minimum of ten (10) questions on their own. Responses are only required if the instructor deems necessary:

1. Q1
2. Q2
3. Q3
4. Q4
5. Q5
6. Q6
7. Q7
8. Q8
9. Q9
10. Q10

Part C

Crime Rate Calculations

Violent Extremist Attacks: 34
Population: 76,887
Crime Rate =

Lastly, the students will upload this final document into your college's Learning Management System, upon completion.

ArcGIS Online

© Leonard Zhukovsky/Shutterstock.com

Synopsis of Lab-Theme

Lab Exercise 25 utilizes the state of New Jersey, as the primary jurisdiction. This map contains data representing crimes against police, as well as horrific line of duty deaths of police officers. Lab Exercise 25 aims to also focus on an approach using Tactical Crime Analysis, due to the nature of the type of the data exhibited, and on the map. NJSP End of Watch is examined.

© lev radin/Shutterstock.com

Table 25

Layer #	Layer Name	Data Type
One	NJSP End of Watch	Crime and Geographic

Operational Lab-Tasks

This map will include geographic and criminal-oriented data, within New Jersey, over a period of time. Temporal and spatial analysis of data is apparent due to the New Jersey State Officers who lost their lives.

Next, the following operational tasks using the capability features of ArcGIS Online will need to be completed, as seen below:

1. Enter NJ in the right toolbar
2. Left Column Toolbar: Click "Add"
3. See Dropdown Menu: Click "Search for Layers"
4. Type: NJSP
   a. Scroll down, then Add the following "Layers":
      1. NJSP End of Watch
5. If necessary, alter the symbol shape and color for this layer, using "Change Style"
6. Review all relevant data for each layer by clicking "Show Table," prior to formulating and submitting your responses

Once all Layers are added, your map should appear as seen below:

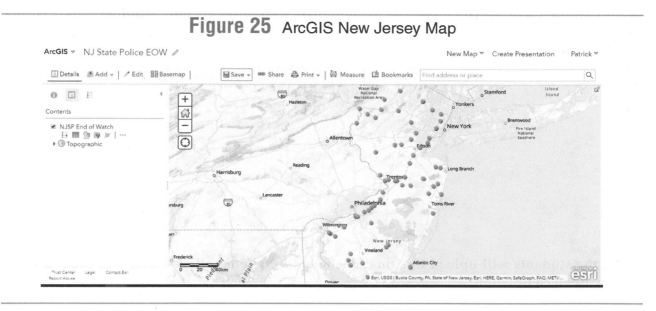

Figure 25 ArcGIS New Jersey Map

Part A

Students will respond accordingly to the following questions on this document, using the data provided.

1. What is the total time frame that this data set covers, in years?
2. What was the cause of death to Trooper Zimmerman in this data?
3. Who was badge number 4575?
4. Who is attributed to the end of watch on May 6, 1984?
5. Who was badge number 5059?
6. Who was ranked as Trooper First Class at their end of watch?
7. Who was badge number 4429?
8. What occurred on Chimney Rock Road?
9. Who was badge number 4718?
10. How many NJSP were murdered causing their end of watch?
11. Who was badge number 4971?
12. Who was badge number 2706?
13. How many motorcycle accidents occurred in this data set?
14. Who was badge number 2753?
15. Who was badge number 3296?

Part B

Students will now perform an in-depth analysis with the current data in the layers uploaded to create a minimum of ten (10) questions on their own. Responses are only required if the instructor deems necessary:

1. Q1
2. Q2
3. Q3
4. Q4
5. Q5
6. Q6
7. Q7
8. Q8
9. Q9
10. Q10

Lastly, the students will upload this final document into your college's Learning Management System, upon completion.

26

ArcGIS Online

© Studio barcelona/Shutterstock.com

Synopsis of Lab-Theme

Lab Exercise 26 utilizes Las Vegas, Nevada, as the primary jurisdiction. This map contains data representing crime and police response. Lab Exercise 26 aims to also focus on an approach using Strategic Crime Analysis, due to the nature of the type of criminal offenders exhibited in the layers, and on the map, as this police agency is one of the busiest in the nation. Las Vegas Metropolitan Polic2 is examined.

© Leonard Zhukovsky/Shutterstock.com

Table 26

Layer #	Layer Name	Data Type
One	Las Vegas Metropolitan Polic2	Crime and Geographic

Operational Lab-Tasks

This map will include geographic and criminal-oriented data, within Las Vegas, as stated. Also, an examination of a multitude of crime is valuable for temporal and spatial analysis.

Next, the following operational tasks using the capability features of ArcGIS Online will need to be completed, as seen below:

1. Enter Las Vegas in the right toolbar
2. Left Column Toolbar: Click "Add"
3. See Dropdown Menu: Click "Search for Layers"
4. Type: Las Vegas police
   a. Scroll down, then add the following "Layers":
      1. Las Vegas Metropolitan Polic2
5. If necessary, alter the symbol shape and color for the layer, using "Change Style"
6. Review all relevant data for each layer by clicking "Show Table," prior to formulating and submitting your responses

Once all Layers are added, your map should appear as seen below:

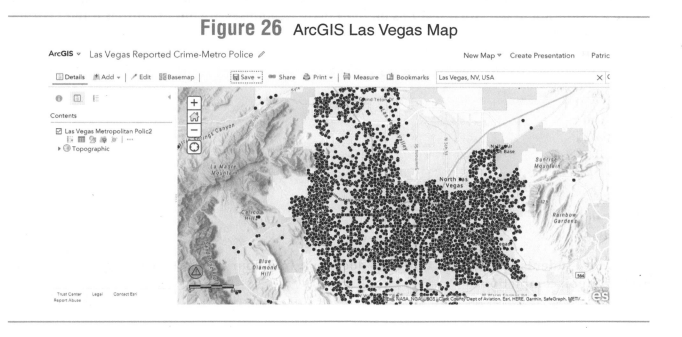

Figure 26 ArcGIS Las Vegas Map

Part A

Students will respond accordingly to the following questions on this document, using the data provided.

1. How many crimes occurred in beat C2?
2. How many crimes are assigned to Ward 6?
3. How many crimes occurred in beat P4?
4. How many crimes are assigned to Ward 3?
5. How many crimes occurred in beat O1?
6. How many crimes occurred in beat X5?
7. How many times did an auto burglary occur?
8. How many crimes occurred in beat P5?
9. How many times was an automobile recovered?
10. How many crimes occurred in beat J4?
11. How many times was an automobile stolen?
12. How many crimes occurred in beat S3?
13. How many times did a robbery occur?
14. How many crimes occurred in beat I3?
15. How many times did some other form of a disturbance occur?
16. How many crimes occurred in beat K1?
17. How many times did an incident occur near Westwind Road?
18. How many crimes occurred in beat R2?
19. How many times did an assault occur?
20. How many crimes occurred in beat R1?

Part B

Students will now perform an in-depth analysis with the current data in the layers uploaded to create a minimum of ten (10) questions on their own. Responses are only required if the instructor deems necessary:

1. Q1
2. Q2
3. Q3
4. Q4
5. Q5
6. Q6
7. Q7
8. Q8
9. Q9
10. Q10

Lastly, the students will upload this final document into your college's Learning Management System, upon completion.

ArcGIS Online

27

© Darwin Brandis/Shutterstock.com

Synopsis of Lab-Theme

Lab Exercise 27 utilizes three states and high-level narcotic manufacturing, as the primary jurisdiction and crime. This map contains layers which include data representing an approach representing Tactical Crime Analysis, based on the criminal activity and clandestine fashion in which it is created. Meth Labs in the City of Tulsa, TN Clan Meth Labs, and DCHD Meth Labs, are examined.

Table 27

Layer #	Layer Name	Data Type
One	Meth Labs in the City of Tulsa	Crime and Geographic
Two	TN Clan Meth Labs	Crime and Geographic
Three	DCHD Meth Labs	Crime and Geographic

Operational Lab-Tasks

This map will include geographic and criminal-oriented data, within the states of Indiana, Oklahoma, and Tennessee. The manufacturing and distribution of methamphetamine is the focus, as well as the illegal laboratories used to create this dilemma within our society. A highlight in spatial analysis is featured.

Next, the following operational tasks using the capability features of ArcGIS Online will need to be completed, as seen below:

1. Enter USA in the right toolbar
2. Left Column Toolbar: Click "Add"
3. See Dropdown Menu: Click "Search for Layers"
4. Type: Meth Labs
    a. Scroll down, then add the following "Layers":
        1. Meth Labs in the City of Tulsa
        2. TN Clan Meth Labs
        3. DCHD Meth Labs
5. If necessary, alter the symbol shape and color for any layer, using "Change Style"
6. Review all relevant data for each layer by clicking "Show Table," prior to formulating and submitting your responses

Once all Layers are added, your map should appear as seen below:

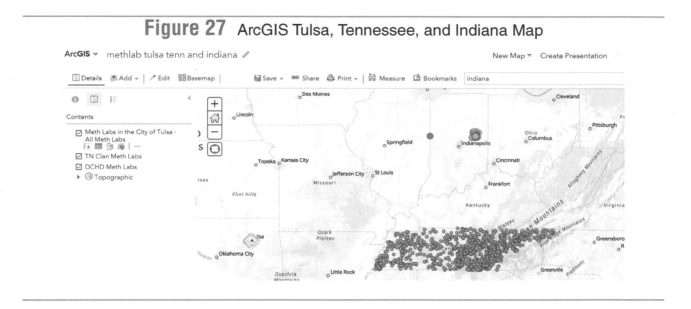

Figure 27 ArcGIS Tulsa, Tennessee, and Indiana Map

Part A

Students will respond accordingly to the following questions on this document, using the data provided.

1. How many meth labs in Indiana were seized from a bedroom?
2. How many meth labs in Indiana were seized from a cabin?
3. How many meth labs in Indiana were seized from a garage?
4. How many meth labs in Indiana were seized from a kitchen?
5. How many meth labs in Indiana were seized from a basement?
6. How many meth labs in Indiana displayed any reactions that were not started?

7. How many meth labs in Tennessee were located on Dutch Valley Road?
8. How many meth labs in Tennessee were located in Crossville?
9. How many meth labs in Tennessee were located across the entire state?
10. How many meth labs in Tennessee were located on Lenoir Loop?
11. How many meth labs in Tennessee were located on Cookeville?
12. How many meth labs in Tennessee were located in Harriman?
13. How many more meth labs were there in Tennessee than Tulsa?
14. How many meth labs in Tulsa were found in 2006?
15. How many meth labs in Tulsa were found in a dump?
16. How many meth labs in Tulsa were found inside a business?
17. How many meth labs in Tulsa were found in 2005?
18. How many meth labs in Tulsa were found within a residence?
19. How many meth labs in Tulsa were considered mobile?
20. How many meth labs in Tulsa were located in a multifamily dwelling?

Part B

Students will now perform an in-depth analysis with the current data in the layers uploaded to create a minimum of ten (10) questions on their own. Responses are only required if the instructor deems necessary:

1. Q1
2. Q2
3. Q3
4. Q4
5. Q5
6. Q6
7. Q7
8. Q8
9. Q9
10. Q10

Part C

Crime Rate Calculations

Apprehensions from Meth Labs: 530 Murders
Population: 65,599
Crime Rate =

Lastly, the students will upload this final document into your college's Learning Management System, upon completion.

ArcGIS Online

28

© Oleh Svetiukha/Shutterstock.com

Synopsis of Lab-Theme

Lab Exercise 28 utilizes the globe, across the world, as the jurisdiction. Lab Exercise 28 aims to also focus on an approach using Strategic Crime Analysis, due to the nature of the type of crime, exhibited in the layers, and on the map. This crime is cocaine trafficking on a global level. Cocaine-Related Corruption, Cocaine Consumption by Country, and Global Cocaine Consumption are examined.

© photopixel/Shutterstock.com

Table 28

Layer #	Layer Name	Data Type
One	Cocaine-Related Corruption	Crime and Geographic
Two	Cocaine Consumption by Country	Crime and Geographic
Three	Global Cocaine Consumption	Crime and Geographic

Operational Lab-Tasks

This map will include geographic and criminal-oriented data, across the globe. Cocaine consumption is examined across various continents, displaying temporal and spatial components.

Next, the following operational tasks using the capability features of ArcGIS Online will need to be completed, as seen below:

1. Enter any continent in the right toolbar
2. Left Column Toolbar: Click "Add"
3. See Dropdown Menu: Click "Search for Layers"
4. Type: Cocaine
   a. Scroll down, then add the following "Layers":
      1. Cocaine-Related Corruption
      2. Cocaine Consumption by Country
      3. Global Cocaine Consumption
5. If necessary, alter the symbol shape and color for any layer, using "Change Style"
6. Review all relevant data for each layer by clicking "Show Table," prior to formulating and submitting your responses

Once all Layers are added, your map should appear as seen below:

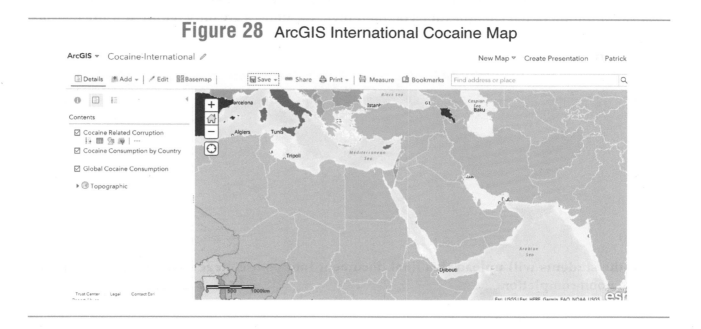

Figure 28 ArcGIS International Cocaine Map

Part A

Students will respond accordingly to the following questions on this document, using the data provided.

1. What is the population of Togo?
2. Does Costa Rica possess cocaine-related corruption?
3. What is the population of Gambia?
4. Is Albania considered a Primary Land-type?
5. How many nations possess a land_rank of 3?
6. Do any very small islands possess a land_rank greater than 1?
7. How many different land_ranks does Bangladesh contain?
8. How many countries does Asia contain within this data set?
9. How many land_ranks does North America possess in this data set?
10. Do people consume cocaine in the British Virgin Islands?

Part B

Students will now perform an in-depth analysis with the current data in the layers uploaded to create a minimum of ten (10) questions on their own. Responses are only required if the instructor deems necessary:

1. Q1
2. Q2
3. Q3
4. Q4
5. Q5
6. Q6
7. Q7
8. Q8
9. Q9
10. Q10

Lastly, the students will upload this final document into your college's Learning Management System, upon completion.

ArcGIS Online

World issues
icon set

poverty and homelessness

hunger

health and well-being

inequality

unemployment

education

water supply

terrorism and war

crime and security

industry and infrastructure

economic issues

infectious diseases

electricity supply

environment and climate

corruption

drug abuse

© TheModernCanvas/Shutterstock.com

Synopsis of Lab-Theme

Lab Exercise 29 utilizes the continent of Africa, as the primary jurisdiction. This map contains data representing a major security threat group across the globe, who often works alongside ISIS and Al-Qaeda. Intelligence analysis is the precursor for this data. Boko Haram Attacks are examined.

Table 29

Layer #	Layer Name	Data Type
One	Boko Haram Attacks	Crime and Geographic

Operational Lab-Tasks

This map will include geographic and criminal-oriented data, within Africa, as stated, whereas Boko Haram often contributes harm and horror in various regions. Spatial and temporal patterns are also explored.

Next, the following operational tasks using the capability features of ArcGIS Online will need to be completed, as seen below:

1. Enter Africa in the right toolbar
2. Left Column Toolbar: Click "Add"
3. See Dropdown Menu: Click "Search for Layers"
4. Type: Terror
   a. Scroll down, then add the following "Layers":
      1. Boko Haram Attacks
5. If necessary, alter the symbol shape and color for this layer, using "Change Style"
6. Review all relevant data for each layer by clicking "Show Table," prior to formulating and submitting your responses

Once all Layers are added, your map should appear as seen below:

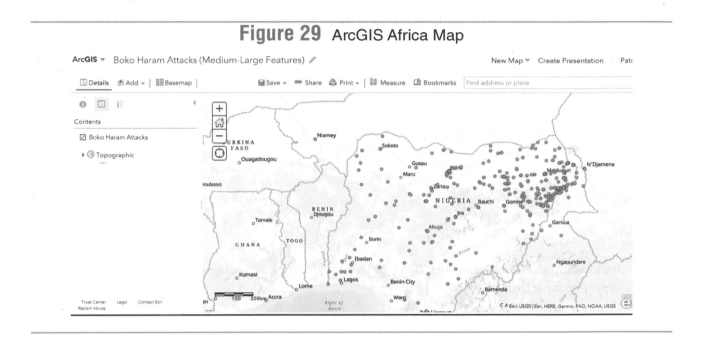

Figure 29 ArcGIS Africa Map

Part A

Students will respond accordingly to the following questions on this document, using the data provided.

1. How many attacks are embedded within this data set?
2. How many hostage-taking incidents occurred, where a Kidnapping ensued?
3. How many incidents used dynamite as a weapon of mass destruction to cause violence?
4. How many incidents targeted Police?
5. How many incidents included exactly 100 fatalities?
6. How many incidents included zero "0" fatalities and zero "0" injuries, simultaneously?
7. How many different groups of perpetrators are there in this data set?
8. How many incidents targeted a Bank?
9. How many total deaths occurred within this data set?
10. How many attacks included a rocket launcher?

Part B

Students will now perform an in-depth analysis with the current data in the layers uploaded to create a minimum of ten (10) questions on their own. Responses are only required if the instructor deems necessary:

1. Q1
2. Q2
3. Q3
4. Q4
5. Q5
6. Q6
7. Q7
8. Q8
9. Q9
10. Q10

Lastly, the students will upload this final document into your college's Learning Management System, upon completion.

ArcGIS Online

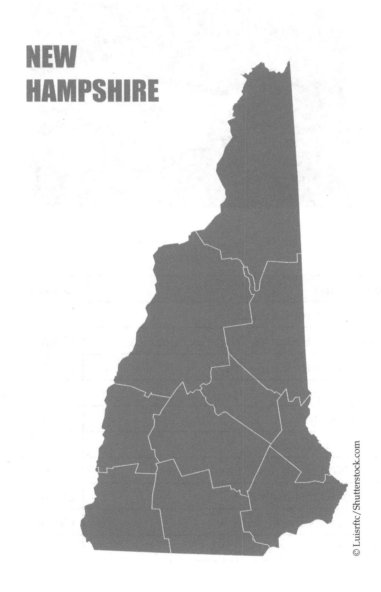

NEW
HAMPSHIRE

Synopsis of Lab-Theme

Lab Exercise 30 utilizes the state of New Hampshire, as the primary jurisdiction. This map contains layers which include data representing multiple crimes across various years, ranging in intensity. Lab Exercise 30 aims to also focus on an approach using Administrative Crime Analysis, due to the nature of the type of crimes, and the amount exhibited in the layers, and on the map. New Hampshire Crime 2018, New Hampshire Crime 2018-All Agencies, New Hampshire Crime 2017, NH Police Agencies, Homicide Offenses, Prostitution Offenses, Murder Non-negligent Manslaughter, Negligent Manslaughter, Murder Justifiable Homicide, and Motor Vehicle Thefts, are examined.

© Cryptographer/Shutterstock.com

Table 30

Layer #	Layer Name	Data Type
One	New Hampshire Crime 2018	Crime
Two	New Hampshire Crime 2018-All Agencies	Crime and Geographic
Three	New Hampshire Crime 2017	Crime
Four	NH Police Agencies	Geographic
Five	Homicide Offenses	Crime
Six	Prostitution Offenses	Crime
Seven	Murder Non-negligent Manslaughter	Crime
Eight	Negligent Manslaughter	Crime
Nine	Murder Justifiable Homicide	Crime
Ten	Motor Vehicle Thefts	Crime

Operational Lab-Tasks

This map will include geographic and criminal-oriented data, within the state of New Hampshire, as stated. The balance of data is highlighted using temporal and spatial analysis, examining highly specific locations and crimes.

Next, the following operational tasks using the capability features of ArcGIS Online will need to be completed, as seen below:

1. Enter New Hampshire in the right toolbar
2. Left Column Toolbar: Click "Add"
3. See Dropdown Menu: Click "Search for Layers"
4. Type: New Hampshire crime
   a. Scroll down, then add the following "Layers":
      1. Sex New Hampshire Crime 2018
      2. New Hampshire Crime 2018-All Agencies
      3. New Hampshire Crime 2017
      4. NH Police Agencies
      5. Homicide Offenses
      6. Prostitution Offenses
      7. Non-negligent Manslaughter
      8. Negligent Manslaughter
      9. Murder Justifiable Homicide
      10. Motor Vehicle Thefts
5. Alter the symbol shape and color for any layer, using "Change Style"
6. Review all relevant data for each layer by clicking "Show Table," prior to formulating and submitting your responses

Once all Layers are added, your map should appear as seen below:

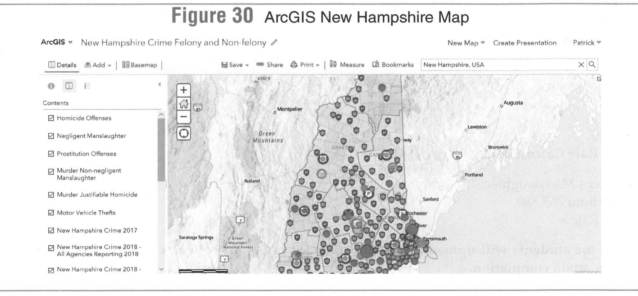

Figure 30 ArcGIS New Hampshire Map

Part A

Students will respond accordingly to the following questions on this document, using the data provided.

1. In 2018, as reported by the State Police in New Hampshire, how many crimes against persons occurred, per this data set?
2. In 2018, as reported by the County Police in New Hampshire, how many crimes against property in Strafford occurred, per this data set?
3. In 2018, as reported by Other Police agencies in New Hampshire, how many total incidents occurred, per this data set?
4. In 2018, as reported by the All Police agencies in New Hampshire, how many total crimes were reported, per this data set?
5. In 2017, as reported in New Hampshire, how many total crimes occurred, per this data set?
6. How many total homicides were reported by Keene Police?
7. How many total Negligent Manslaughter incidents were reported by Manchester Police?
8. How many prostitution offenses were reported by the Laconia Police?
9. How many sexual assaults with an object were reported by the Alton Police?
10. How many robberies were reported by the Belmont Police?

Part B

Students will now perform an in-depth analysis with the current data in the layers uploaded to create a minimum of ten (10) questions on their own. Responses are only required if the instructor deems necessary:

1. Q1
2. Q2
3. Q3
4. Q4
5. Q5
6. Q6
7. Q7
8. Q8
9. Q9
10. Q10

Part C

Crime Rate Calculations

Negligent Manslaughter: 432
Population: 765,880
Crime Rate =

Lastly, the students will upload this final document into your college's Learning Management System, upon completion.

ArcGIS Online

© SevenMaps/Shutterstock.com

Synopsis of Lab-Theme

Lab Exercise 31 utilizes the state of California, and the city of Compton, as the primary jurisdiction. This map contains layers which include data representing drug crime counts or incidents, and how the spatial aspect of crud crimes committed near or at schools in that city, is the focus. Lab Exercise 31 aims to also focus on an approach using Strategic Crime Analysis, due to the nature of the type of criminal offender exhibited in the layers, and on the map. Drug Crimes Summarized, Drug Crime Count bath wards with enrichment, and Bath drugs crime data by ward enriched v2, are examined.

© sacolor/Shutterstock.com

Table 31

Layer #	Layer Name	Data Type
One	Drug Crimes Summarized	Crime and Geographic
Two	Drug Crime Count bath wards with enrichment	Crime and Geographic
Three	Bath drugs crime data by ward enriched v2	Crime and Geographic

Operational Lab-Tasks

This map will include geographic and criminal-oriented data, within the city of Compton. Also, drug crimes within a specific distance from schools are utilized, highlighting spatial feature, as discussed, as well as temporal patterns, are to be explored.

Next, the following operational tasks using the capability features of ArcGIS Online will need to be completed, as seen below:

1. Enter Compton, California in the right toolbar
2. Left Column Toolbar: Click "Add"
3. See Dropdown Menu: Click "Search for Layers"
4. Type: Drug Crimes
   a. Scroll down, then add the following "Layers":
      1. Drug Crimes Summarized
      2. Drug Crime Count bath wards with enrichment
      3. Bath drugs crime data by ward enriched v2
5. Alter the symbol shape and color for any layer, using "Change Style"
6. Review all relevant data for each layer by clicking "Show Table," prior to formulating and submitting your responses

Once all Layers are added, your map should appear as seen below:

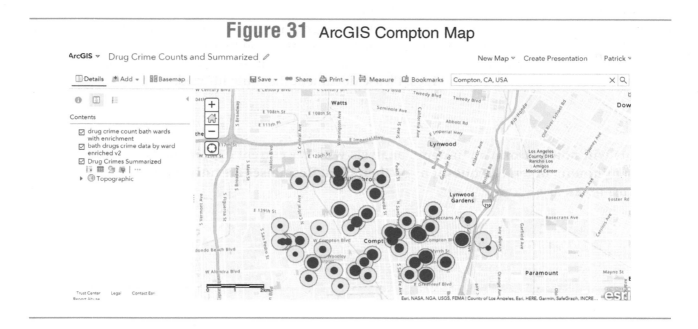

Figure 31 ArcGIS Compton Map

Part A

Students will respond accordingly to the following questions on this document, using the data provided.

1. How many elementary schools are listed within this data set? It must state elementary.
2. How many schools included in this data set possess 62 to 130 drug crimes?
3. How many schools included in this data set possess 32 to 61 drug crimes?
4. How many schools included in this data set possess 18 to 31 drug crimes?
5. How many schools included in this data set possess 9 to 17 drug crimes?
6. How many schools included in this data set possess 1 to 8 drug crimes?
7. How many middle schools are listed within this data set? It must state middle.
8. How many high schools are listed within this data set? It must state high school.
9. What is the proximity between the locations where the count of points is 14? Please document an actual route.
10. What is the proximity between the locations where the count of points is 40? No routes needed.
11. What is the proximity for the two counts of point-locations, where the total students are 439? No routes needed.
12. Does Bunche Middle School possess the most drug crimes is this data set? Then who does?
13. What is the proximity between the two counts of points where the schools are named after Roosevelt? No routes
14. What is the proximity between the two counts of points where the schools possess over 2,000 students? No routes
15. What is the proximity between the three counts of points where the schools possess over 1,000 students but less than 2,000? No routes needed.

16. How many total students are included in this data set, where a "school name" is attached only?
17. How many students are middle schools only?
18. How many students are high school students?
19. Is there a school location, where if you click its geographic location on the map, it is duplicated with another school name? (Two different names, one point on map)
20. Document the farthest possible distance from one school to the other, within this data set. Name the schools and the distance in Miles. Please document the route utilized.

Part B

Students will now perform an in-depth analysis with the current data in the layers uploaded to create a minimum of ten (10) questions on their own. Responses are only required if the instructor deems necessary:

1. Q1
2. Q2
3. Q3
4. Q4
5. Q5
6. Q6
7. Q7
8. Q8
9. Q9
10. Q10

Lastly, the students will upload this final document into your college's Learning Management System, upon completion.

ArcGIS Online

© TTstudio/Shutterstock.com

Synopsis of Lab-Theme

Lab Exercise 32 utilizes the city of New York, as the primary jurisdiction. This map contains layers which include data representing police-oriented geographic data. Lab Exercise 32 aims to also focus on an approach using Administrative Crime Analysis, due to the nature of the data exhibited in the layers, and on the map. NYPD Precincts and NYPD Sectors are examined.

© Photo Spirit/Shutterstock.com

Table 32

Layer #	Layer Name	Data Type
One	NYPD Precincts	Geographic
Two	NYPD Sectors	Geographic

Operational Lab-Tasks

This map will include geographic data within the state of New York, specifically, the five boroughs of New York City. Spatial analysis is a focal point for this data. NYPD Precincts and NYPD Sectors are examined.

Next, the following operational tasks using the capability features of ArcGIS Online will need to be completed, as seen below:

1. Enter NYC in the right toolbar
2. Left Column Toolbar: Click "Add"
3. See Dropdown Menu: Click "Search for Layers"
4. Type: NYPD
   a. Scroll down, then add the following "Layers":
      1. NYPD Precincts
      2. NYPD Sectors
5. Alter the symbol shape and color for any layer, using "Change Style"
6. Review all relevant data for each layer by clicking "Show Table," prior to formulating and submitting your responses

Once all Layers are added, your map should appear as seen below:

Figure 32 ArcGIS New York City Map

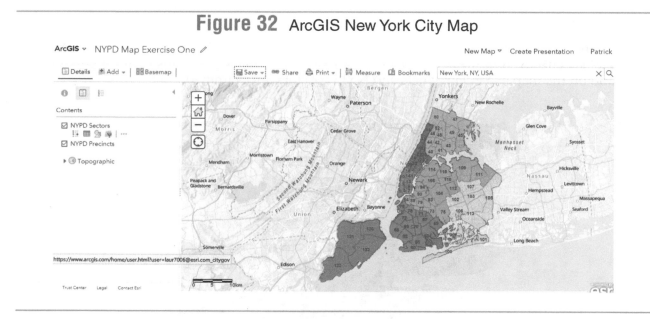

Part A

Students will respond accordingly to the following questions on this document, using the data provided.

1. How many total sectors, relevant to NYPD jurisdictions, are within this data set?
2. How many sectors comprise the 43rd Precinct?
3. How many sectors comprise the 45th Precinct
4. How many square miles is sector 6H?
5. How many sectors comprise the 6th Precinct?
6. How many square miles is sector 6F?
7. How many sectors comprise the 68th Precinct?
8. How many square miles is sector 66E?
9. How many sectors comprise the 61st Precinct?
10. How many square miles is sector 6I?
11. How many sectors comprise the 75th Precinct?
12. How many square miles is sector 78A?
13. How many sectors comprise the 50th Precinct?
14. How many square miles is sector 34B?
15. How many sectors comprise the 34th Precinct?
16. How many square miles is sector 41B?
17. How many sectors comprise the 44th Precinct?
18. How many square miles is sector 46A?
19. How many sectors comprise the 43rd Precinct?
20. How many square miles is sector 32A?
21. How many sectors comprise the 30th Precinct?
22. How many sectors comprise the 19th Precinct?
23. How many sectors comprise the 18th Precinct?
24. How many sectors comprise the 12th Precinct?
25. How many square miles is sector 50E?
26. How many sectors comprise the 42nd Precinct?
27. How many sectors comprise the 41st Precinct?
28. How many sectors comprise the 45th Precinct?
29. How many square miles is sector 17D?
30. How many sectors comprise the 17th Precinct?
31. How many square miles is sector 28D?
32. How many sectors comprise the 78th Precinct?
33. How many square miles is sector 104A?
34. How many sectors comprise the 7th Precinct?
35. How many square miles is sector 102C?

Part B

Students will now perform an in-depth analysis with the current data in the layers uploaded to create a minimum of ten (10) questions on their own. Responses are only required if the instructor deems necessary:

1. Q1
2. Q2
3. Q3
4. Q4
5. Q5
6. Q6
7. Q7
8. Q8
9. Q9
10. Q10

Lastly, the students will upload this final document into your college's Learning Management System, upon completion.

ArcGIS Online

© rblfmr/Shutterstock.com

Synopsis of Lab-Theme

Lab Exercise 33 utilizes the city of New York, as the primary jurisdiction. This map contains layers which include data representing highly specific statistics which in turn, were used in federal court cases. Lab Exercise 33 aims to also focus on an approach using Administrative Crime Analysis, due to the nature of the type of data exhibited in the layers, and on the map. Stop and Frisk 2018 WFL1-Precinct_Boundary, Stop and Frisk 2018 WFL1-2018 Stop Rate for Young Adults, Stop and Frisk 2018 WFL1-2018 Stop Rate for White People, Stop and Frisk 2018 WFL1-2018 Stop Rate for Hispanic People, Stop and Frisk 2018 WFL1-2018 Stop Rate for Black People, Stop and Frisk 2018 WFL1-2018 Arrest Rate by Precinct, and Stop and Frisk 2018 WFL1-2018 Stops by Precinct, are examined.

Table 33

Layer #	Layer Name	Data Type
One	Stop and Frisk 2018 WFL1-Precinct_Boundary	Geographic
Two	Stop and Frisk 2018 WFL1-2018 Stop Rate for Young Adults	Crime and Geographic
Three	Stop and Frisk 2018 WFL1-2018 Stop Rate for White People	Crime and Geographic
Four	Stop and Frisk 2018 WFL1-2018 Stop Rate for Hispanic People	Crime and Geographic
Five	Stop and Frisk 2018 WFL1-2018 Stop Rate for Black People	Crime and Geographic
Six	Stop and Frisk 2018 WFL1-2018 Arrest Rate by Precinct	Crime and Geographic
Seven	Stop and Frisk 2018 WFL1-2018 Stops by Precinct	Geographic

Operational Lab-Tasks

This map will include geographic and criminal-oriented data, within the New York City. A multitude of data is to be examined, where the foundation is statistical data which served as evidence in court, due to a variety of legal matters.

Next, the following operational tasks using the capability features of ArcGIS Online will need to be completed, as seen below:

1. Enter NYC in the right toolbar
2. Left Column Toolbar: Click "Add"
3. See Dropdown Menu: Click "Search for Layers"
4. Type: NYPD
   a. Scroll down, then add the following "Layers":
      1. Sex Stop and Frisk 2018 WFL1-Precinct_Boundary
      2. Stop and Frisk 2018 WFL1-2018 Stop Rate for Young Adults
      3. Stop and Frisk 2018 WFL1-2018 Stop Rate for White People
      4. Stop and Frisk 2018 WFL1-2018 Stop Rate for Hispanic People

    5. Stop and Frisk 2018 WFL1-2018 Stop Rate for Black People

    6. Stop and Frisk 2018 WFL1-2018 Arrest Rate by Precinct

    7. Stop and Frisk 2018 WFL1-2018 Stops by Precinct

5. If necessary, alter the symbol shape and color for any layer, using "Change Style"

6. Review all relevant data for each layer by clicking "Show Table," prior to formulating and submitting your responses

Once all Layers are added, your map should appear as seen below:

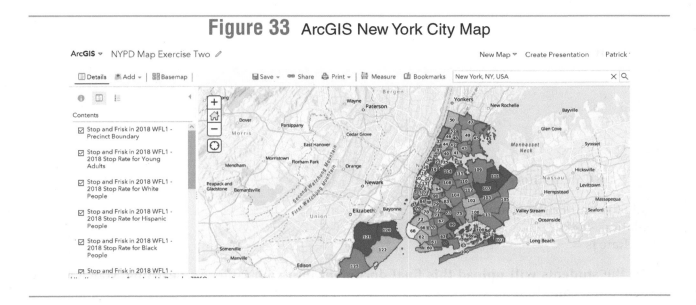

Figure 33 ArcGIS New York City Map

Part A

Students will respond accordingly to the following questions on this document, using the data provided.

1. In 2018, how many young adults in NYC were arrested after a stop and frisk?

2. In 2018, how many young adults who were documented as Hispanic in NYC were stopped and frisked?

3. Which precinct possessed the least amount of arrests for White people who were stopped and frisked?

4. In 2018, which precinct possessed the most incidents of stop and frisk?

5. In 2018, how many young adults in NYC were arrested after a stop and frisk in the 41st Precinct?

6. In 2018, how many young adults who were documented as White were stopped and frisked?

7. Which precinct possessed the most amount of arrests for Black people who were stopped and frisked?

8. In 2018, which precinct possessed the least number of incidents of stop and frisk?

9. In 2018, how many young adults in NYC were under 25 years old?

10. In 2018, how many young adults who were documented as Black in NYC were stopped and frisked?

Part B

Students will now perform an in-depth analysis with the current data in the layers uploaded to create a minimum of ten (10) questions on their own. Responses are only required if the instructor deems necessary:

1. Q1
2. Q2
3. Q3
4. Q4
5. Q5
6. Q6
7. Q7
8. Q8
9. Q9
10. Q10

Part C

Crime Rate Calculations

Illegal Stop and Frisks conducted: 35
Population: 4887
Crime Rate is =

Lastly, the students will upload this final document into your college's Learning Management System, upon completion.

ArcGIS Online

© spyarm/Shutterstock.com

Synopsis of Lab-Theme

Lab Exercise 34 utilizes the city of New York, as the primary jurisdiction. Lab Exercise 34 aims to also focus on an approach using Strategic Crime Analysis, due to the nature of the type of crimes exhibited in the layers, and on the map. NYCArrests2018 is examined.

Table 34

Layer #	Layer Name	Data Type
One	NYCArrests2018	Crime and Geographic

Operational Lab-Tasks

This map will include geographic and criminal-oriented data, within the city of New York, as stated. Temporal analysis is the primary aspect followed by spatial components contributing to various incidents.

Next, the following operational tasks using the capability features of ArcGIS Online will need to be completed, as seen below:

1. Enter NYC in the right toolbar
2. Left Column Toolbar: Click "Add"
3. See Dropdown Menu: Click "Search for Layers"
4. Type: NYPD
   a. Scroll down, then add the following "Layers":
      1. NYCArrests2018
5. If necessary, alter the symbol shape and color for this layer, using "Change Style"
6. Review all relevant data for each layer by clicking "Show Table," prior to formulating and submitting your responses

Once all Layers are added, your map should appear as seen below:

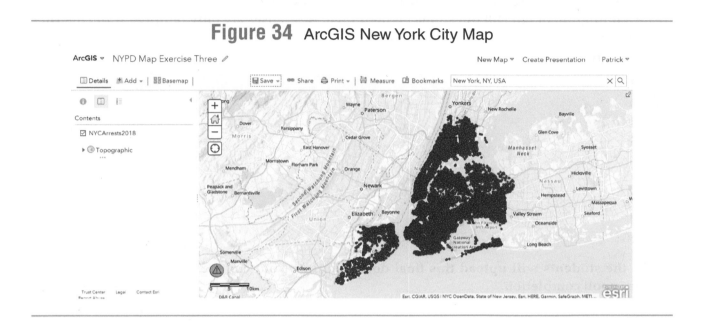

Figure 34 ArcGIS New York City Map

Part A

Students will respond accordingly to the following questions on this document, using the data provided.

1. How many arrests were made by police in 2018, per this data set?
2. How many arrests were made by police in June 2018?
3. In 2018, how many incidents of intoxicated driving occurred?
4. In 2018, how many times did someone commit forgery?
5. In 2018, how many times did someone commit felony assault?
6. In 2018, how many times did someone possess dangerous drugs?
7. In 2018, how many total unclassified misdemeanors occurred?
8. In 2018, how many times did someone commit robbery?
9. In 2018, how many times did someone resist arrest?
10. In 2018, how many times did someone not obey traffic laws?

Part B

Students will now perform an in-depth analysis with the current data in the layers uploaded to create a minimum of ten (10) questions on their own. Responses are only required if the instructor deems necessary:

1. Q1
2. Q2
3. Q3
4. Q4
5. Q5
6. Q6
7. Q7
8. Q8
9. Q9
10. Q10

Lastly, the students will upload this final document into your college's Learning Management System, upon completion.

ArcGIS Online

© Kursat Unsal/Shutterstock.com

Synopsis of Lab-Theme

Lab Exercise 35 utilizes the city of Philadelphia, as the primary jurisdiction. Lab Exercise 35 aims to focus on an approach using Intelligence Crime Analysis, due to the nature of the type of criminal offender exhibited in the layers, and on the map. Gang Territories and Gang Members are examined.

© golubovystock/Shutterstock.com

Table 35

Layer #	Layer Name	Data Type
One	Gang Territories	Geographic
Two	Gang Members	Crime and Geographic

Operational Lab-Tasks

This map will include geographic and criminal-oriented data, within the city of Philadelphia, as stated. Security threat group members and their jurisdictions are examined alongside the spatial analysis to be conducted.

Next, the following operational tasks using the capability features of ArcGIS Online will need to be completed, as seen below:

1. Enter Philadelphia in the right toolbar
2. Left Column Toolbar: Click "Add"
3. See Dropdown Menu: Click "Search for Layers"
4. Type: Gangs
    a. Scroll down, then add the following "Layers":
        1. Gang Territories
        2. Gang Members
5. Alter the symbol shape and color for any layer, using "Change Style"
6. Review all relevant data for each layer by clicking "Show Table," prior to formulating and submitting your responses

Once all Layers are added, your map should appear as seen below:

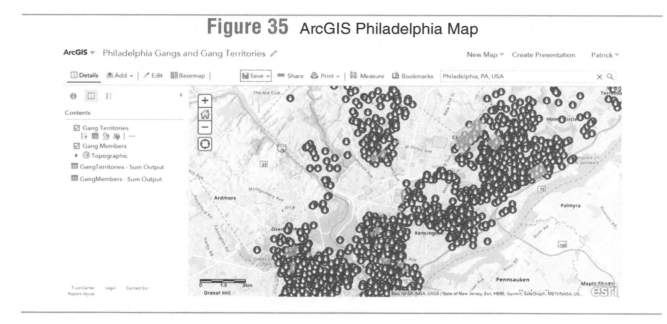

Figure 35   ArcGIS Philadelphia Map

Part A

Students will respond accordingly to the following questions on this document, using the data provided.

1. Does Trez Coleman possess any warrants?
2. Do the True Goons reside in Philadelphia?
3. How many total gang territories exist in Philadelphia?
4. How many Northeast gang territories exist?
5. How many total districts exist within all gang territories?
6. How many gang members are on parole?
7. How many gang members are on probation?
8. How many gang members were born before 1994?
9. How many members are down with BG Crip Click?
10. How many gang members are over 5 ft 9 in height?

Part B

Students will now perform an in-depth analysis with the current data in the layers uploaded to create a minimum of ten (10) questions on their own. Responses are only required if the instructor deems necessary:

1. Q1
2. Q2
3. Q3
4. Q4
5. Q5
6. Q6
7. Q7
8. Q8
9. Q9
10. Q10

Lastly, the students will upload this final document into your college's Learning Management System, upon completion.

ArcGIS Online

© Per Bengtsson/Shutterstock.com

Synopsis of Lab-Theme

Lab Exercise 36 utilizes the state of New Jersey, as the primary jurisdiction. Lab Exercise 36 aims to also focus on an approach using Intelligence Crime Analysis, due to the nature of the type of criminal offender exhibited in the layers, and on the map. 2010 New Jersey Gang Survey is examined.

Table 36

Layer #	Layer Name	Data Type
One	2010 New Jersey Gang Survey	Crime and Geographic

Operational Lab-Tasks

This map will include geographic and criminal-oriented data, within the state of New Jersey. Security threat group members, within this jurisdiction, are the primary data feature. Also, an analysis of spatial features is the focal point.

Next, the following operational tasks using the capability features of ArcGIS Online will need to be completed, as seen below:

1. Enter NJ in the right toolbar
2. Left Column Toolbar: Click "Add"
3. See Dropdown Menu: Click "Search for Layers"
4. Type: Gangs
   a. Scroll down, then add the following "Layers":
      1. 2010 New Jersey Gang Survey
5. Alter the symbol shape and color for this layer, using "Change Style"
6. Review all relevant data for each layer by clicking "Show Table," prior to formulating and submitting your responses

Once all Layers are added, your map should appear as seen below:

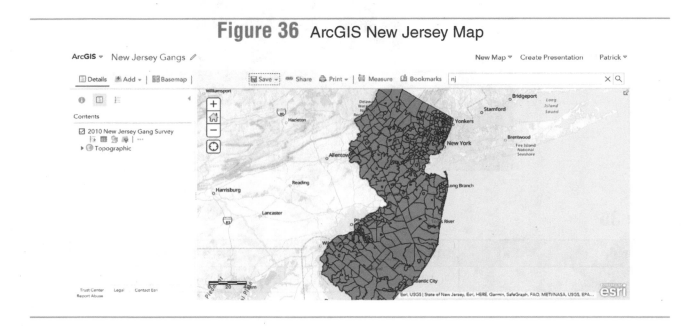

Figure 36 ArcGIS New Jersey Map

Part A

Students will respond accordingly to the following questions on this document, using the data provided.

1. How many Gangs are mentioned in this Layer?
2. How many police departments?
3. Are there any gangs mentioned from West Orange, New Jersey?
4. Which county possesses the most Gang Presence in total (multiple columns?)?
5. Which county possesses the most Sets of Bloods (it must say bloods within the term, and can be coupled with a "set" of the gang as well)?
6. Which county possesses the most Gang Awareness?
7. What is the most heavily populated town as of 2010?
8. What gang is the densest (most prevalent) in relation to the 2010 Population for Counties?
9. What town possesses most square miles in total?
10. How many towns are the Latin Kings within in this state?
11. How many counties are the Pagans within?
12. What gang set is located in Farmingdale, New Jersey?
13. How many Crip Sets are in this Layer?
14. Name at least two of the Crip Sets within this data set
15. Name two areas where any two Crip Gang sets reside within Philadelphia?

Part B

Students will now perform an in-depth analysis with the current data in the layers uploaded to create a minimum of ten (10) questions on their own. Responses are only required if the instructor deems necessary:

1. Q1
2. Q2
3. Q3
4. Q4
5. Q5
6. Q6
7. Q7
8. Q8
9. Q9
10. Q10

Lastly, the students will upload this final document into your college's Learning Management System, upon completion.

ArcGIS Online

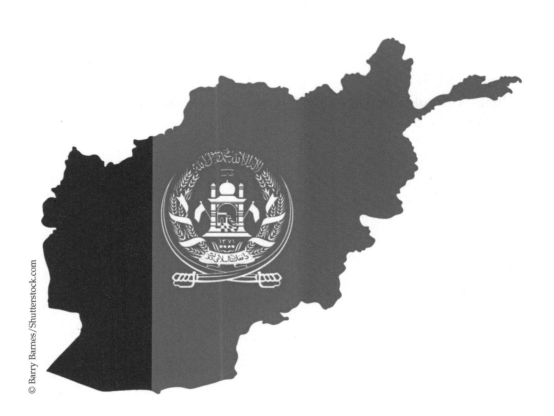

© Barry Barnes/Shutterstock.com

Synopsis of Lab-Theme

Lab Exercise 37 utilizes the nation of Afghanistan, as the primary jurisdiction. This map contains layers which include data representing international terror events confined to this region, coupled with clusters of attacks committed within this nation. Lab Exercise 31 aims to also focus on an approach using Intelligence Crime Analysis, due to the nature of the type of crimes exhibited in the layers, and on the map. Hot Spots Afghanistan Terrorism and Afghanistan Terrorism View, are examined.

© Cube29/Shutterstock.com

Table 37

Layer #	Layer Name	Data Type
One	Hot Spots Afghanistan Terrorism	Crime and Geographic
Two	Afghanistan Terrorism View	Crime and Geographic

Operational Lab-Tasks

This map will include geographic and criminal-oriented data, within the nation of Afghanistan. Temporal aspects of incidents, coupled with spatial features, are utilized.

Next, the following operational tasks using the capability features of ArcGIS Online will need to be completed, as seen below:

1. Enter Afghanistan in the right toolbar
2. Left Column Toolbar: Click "Add"
3. See Dropdown Menu: Click "Search for Layers"
4. Type: Terror
   a. Scroll down, then add the following "Layers":
      1. Hot Spots Afghanistan Terrorism
      2. Afghanistan Terrorism View
5. Alter the symbol shape and color for any layer, using "Change Style"
6. Review all relevant data for each layer by clicking "Show Table," prior to formulating and submitting your responses

Once all Layers are added, your map should appear as seen below:

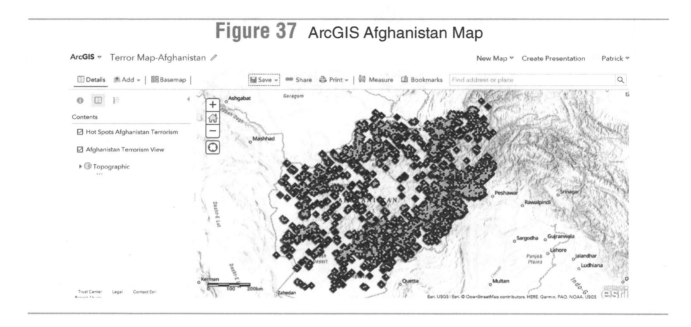

Figure 37 ArcGIS Afghanistan Map

Part A

Students will respond accordingly to the following questions on this document, using the data provided.

1. How many total hotspots exist within this data set?
2. How many hotspots are statistically significant?
3. How many hotspots are not statistically significant?
4. How many hotspots possess a number of points less than 18?
5. How many hotspots possess a number of points less than 11?
6. How many hotspots possess a number of points less than 2?
7. How many hotspots possess a number of points less than 9?
8. How many hotspots possess a number of points more than 5?
9. How many hotspots possess a number of points less than 30?
10. How many hotspots possess a number of points more than 20?
11. How many multiple incidents occurred with Dwah Mande?
12. How many suicide bombers were in Khost?
13. How many total incidents occurred in Gardez?
14. How many successful incidents occurred in Taran Kot?
15. How many successful incidents occurred in Afghan Tapa?

Part B

Students will now perform an in-depth analysis with the current data in the layers uploaded to create a minimum of ten (10) questions on their own. Responses are only required if the instructor deems necessary:

1. Q1
2. Q2
3. Q3
4. Q4
5. Q5
6. Q6
7. Q7
8. Q8
9. Q9
10. Q10

Lastly, the students will upload this final document into your college's Learning Management System, upon completion.

ArcGIS Online

Synopsis of Lab-Theme

Lab Exercise 38 utilizes the United States as the overarching, and primary, jurisdiction. This map contains layers which include data representing highly specific terror incidents due to home grown or other types of attacks. MassShootings2018WithTime and Aggregation of MassShootings 2018 to State Boundaries, are examined.

Table 38

Layer #	Layer Name	Data Type
One	MassShootings2018WithTime	Crime and Geographic
Two	Aggregation of MassShootings 2018 to State Boundaries	Crime and Geographic

Operational Lab-Tasks

This map will include geographic and criminal-oriented data, within the United States, specifically high-profile domestic terror incidents. Also, temporal and spatial features are a focal point.

Next, the following operational tasks using the capability features of ArcGIS Online will need to be completed, as seen below:

1. Enter USA in the right toolbar
2. Left Column Toolbar: Click "Add"
3. See Dropdown Menu: Click "Search for Layers"
4. Type: Terror or mass shootings
   a. Scroll down, then add the following "Layers":
      1. MassShootings2018WithTime
      2. Aggregation of MassShootings 2018 to State Boundaries
5. Alter the symbol shape and color for any layer, using "Change Style"
6. Review all relevant data for each layer by clicking "Show Table," prior to formulating and submitting your responses

Once all Layers are added, your map should appear as seen below:

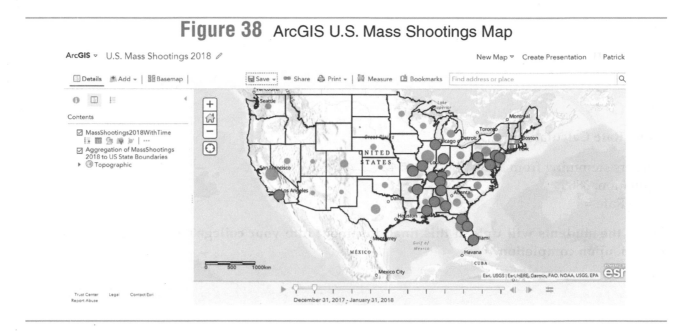

Figure 38 ArcGIS U.S. Mass Shootings Map

Part A

Students will respond accordingly to the following questions on this document, using the data provided.

1. Which state contains the most mass shootings within this data set?
2. How many incidents included more than one shooter?
3. List all mass shooters by last name.
4. Which month had the most shootings overall, regardless of year?
5. How many mass shootings occurred in New York?
6. Which state contained the least amount of mass shootings within this data set?
7. Which mass shooter possesses the most confirmed kills within this data set?
8. How many incidents were committed by only one shooter?
9. Which region of the nation included the most shootings (East Coast, West Coast, Midwest, Southern, or Pacific Northwest)?
10. How many total shooters were from California, per this data?

Part B

Students will now perform an in-depth analysis with the current data in the layers uploaded to create a minimum of ten (10) questions on their own. Responses are only required if the instructor deems necessary:

1. Q1
2. Q2
3. Q3
4. Q4
5. Q5
6. Q6
7. Q7
8. Q8
9. Q9
10. Q10

Part C

Crime Rate Calculations

Murders stemming from Mass Shootings: 42
Population: 3885
Crime Rate =

Lastly, the students will upload this final document into your college's Learning Management System, upon completion.

ArcGIS Online

© Alexander Lukatskiy/Shutterstock.com

Synopsis of Lab-Theme

Lab Exercise 39 utilizes the state of Utah, as the primary jurisdiction. This map contains layers which include data representing crime incidents, and other reported crime which occurred near institutions of learning. Strategic Crime Analysis is a focal point based on the data utilized. SchoolsNearIncidents and SLCPD Crime2018 are examined.

© welcomia/Shutterstock.com

Table 39

Layer #	Layer Name	Data Type
One	SchoolsNearIncidents	Crime and Geographic
Two	SLCPD Crime2018	Crime and Geographic

Operational Lab-Tasks

This map will include geographic and criminal-oriented data, within the state of Utah. Also, reported crime by a large police agency is examined, coupled with spatial aspects focusing on specific distances from schools, are utilized.

Next, the following operational tasks using the capability features of ArcGIS Online will need to be completed, as seen below:

1. Enter Utah in the right toolbar
2. Left Column Toolbar: Click "Add"
3. See Dropdown Menu: Click "Search for Layers"
4. Type: Utah crime
   a. Scroll down, then add the following "Layers":
      1. Sex SchoolsNearIncidents
      2. SLCPD Crime2018
5. Alter the symbol shape and color for any layer, using "Change Style"
6. Review all relevant data for each layer by clicking "Show Table," prior to formulating and submitting your responses

Once all Layers are added, your map should appear as seen below:

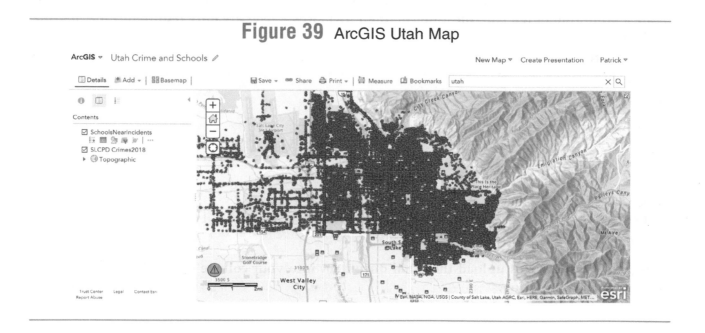

Figure 39 ArcGIS Utah Map

Part A

Students will respond accordingly to the following questions on this document, using the data provided.

1. How many schools were near crime incidents, according to this data?
2. How many cities are represented within this data set?
3. How many counties are represented within this data set?
4. How many Montessori schools are exhibited within this data set?
5. How many Middle schools are exhibited within this data set?
6. Which school possesses a population of 376?
7. Which schools are located in Draper?
8. How many campuses does Summit Academy possess?
9. How many times was Fraud committed within this data set?
10. How many offenses were committed on a Tuesday?

Part B

Students will now perform an in-depth analysis with the current data in the layers uploaded to create a minimum of ten (10) questions on their own. Responses are only required if the instructor deems necessary:

1. Q1
2. Q2
3. Q3
4. Q4
5. Q5
6. Q6
7. Q7
8. Q8
9. Q9
10. Q10

Lastly, the students will upload this final document into your college's Learning Management System, upon completion.

ArcGIS Online

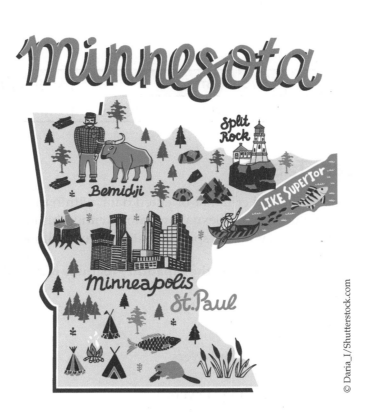

© Daria_I/Shutterstock.com

Synopsis of Lab-Theme

Lab Exercise 40 utilizes the state of Minnesota, as the primary jurisdiction. Lab Exercise 40 aims to also focus on an approach using Strategic Crime Analysis, due to the nature of the type of criminal offender exhibited in the layers, and on the map.

© niroworld/Shutterstock.com

Table 40

Layer #	Layer Name	Data Type
One	Police Incidents 2018 PIMS	Crime and Geographic

Operational Lab-Tasks

This map will include geographic and criminal-oriented data, within the state of Florida, in particular the city of Miami, and its subsections. Sexual predators within this jurisdiction are the primary data feature. Also, Sexual Predators within a specific distance from schools are utilized.

Next, the following operational tasks using the capability features of ArcGIS Online will need to be completed, as seen below:

1. Enter Minnesota in the right toolbar
2. Left Column Toolbar: Click "Add"
3. See Dropdown Menu: Click "Search for Layers"
4. Type: Minnesota police
   a. Scroll down, then add the following "Layers":
      1. Police Incidents 2018 PIMS
5. Alter the symbol shape and color for this layer, using "Change Style"
6. Review all relevant data for each layer by clicking "Show Table," prior to formulating and submitting your responses

Once all Layers are added, your map should appear as seen below:

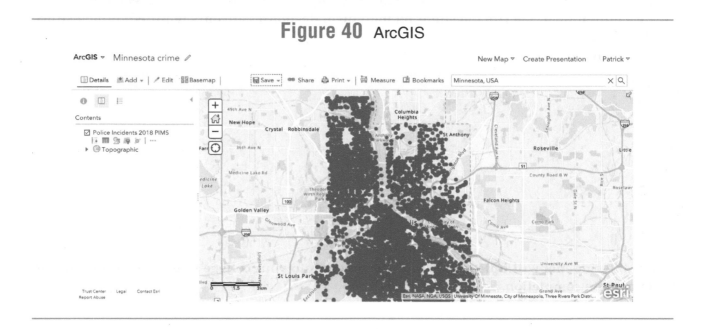

Figure 40 ArcGIS

Part A

Students will respond accordingly to the following questions on this document, using the data provided.

1. How many total police precincts exist within this data set?
2. Which month in 2018 contained the most crime in this data set?
3. How many categories of offenses are exhibited within this data set?
4. Which UCR Code is represented the most in this data set?
5. How many times did a first-degree crime occur within this data set?
6. Which offense is observed the most within this data set?
7. How many neighborhoods exist within this data set?
8. Which precinct is the busiest, according to this data set?
9. How many offenses included a motor vehicle, based on this data?
10. How many times was an offense committed in Elliot Park?

Part B

Students will now perform an in-depth analysis with the current data in the layers uploaded to create a minimum of ten (10) questions on their own. Responses are only required if the instructor deems necessary:

1. Q1
2. Q2
3. Q3
4. Q4
5. Q5
6. Q6
7. Q7
8. Q8
9. Q9
10. Q10

Lastly, the students will upload this final document into your college's Learning Management System, upon completion.